MIRACLES
and
BLESSINGS

MIRACLES *and* BLESSINGS

W. Jeffrey Marsh
Ron R. Munns

BOOKCRAFT
Salt Lake City, Utah

Stories on pages 6–7, 52–54, 76–77, 85–87, 89–91, 94–96, 97–98, 111–12, 120–21, and 125–26 are owned by The Church of Jesus Christ of Latter-day Saints and are used by permission.

Library of Congress Catalog Card Number: 93-74580
ISBN 0-88494-915-X

First Printing, 1994

Printed in the United States of America

Contents

Introduction

Having heard his father speak of marvelous visions, Nephi desired to have similar experiences:

> And it came to pass after I, Nephi, having heard all the words of my father, concerning the things which he saw in a vision, and also the things which he spake by the power of the Holy Ghost, which power he received by faith on the Son of God—and the Son of God was the Messiah who should come—I, Nephi, was desirous also that I might see, and hear, and know of these things, by the power of the Holy Ghost, which is the gift of God unto all those who diligently seek him, as well in times of old as in the time that he should manifest himself unto the children of men.
>
> For he is the same yesterday, to-day, and forever; and the way is prepared for all men from the foundation of the world, if it so be that they repent and come unto him.
>
> For he that diligently seeketh shall find; and the mysteries of God shall be unfolded unto them, by the power of the Holy Ghost, as well in these times as in times of old, and as well in times of old as in times to come; wherefore, the course of the Lord is one eternal round. (1 Nephi 10:17–19.)

The scriptures contain a rich treasury of inspiring and faith-promoting stories. They introduce us to real characters who serve as examples of what we ought to be and how we ought to act.

The same kinds of spiritual experiences that transpired anciently are happening among the faithful today. These modern-day stories provide valuable resources for teaching and witnessing to the verity of the scriptural truth that "the course of the Lord is one eternal round."

The Value of Using Good Stories

Elder Boyd K. Packer taught about the important role stories can play in touching lives: they help us transfer gospel principles into daily practices. "In our teaching, stories . . . can help make powerful points. As we feed those for whom we are responsible, at home or in the classroom, may we search out stories that are relevant and unforgettable, and help our youth relate saving gospel truths to their everyday lives." (*Teach Ye Diligently* [Salt Lake City: Deseret Book Co., 1975], pp. 253–54.)

The Savior often used stories, analogies, and parables in his teaching. Undoubtedly one reason he did so was that stories can teach and reach every person on his or her own level. They become sentence sermons and spiritual time bombs that can go off in our memory when we need them most. Elder Packer pointed out how effective stories can be in teaching others:

> If you have a group to teach and it is a large group, determine beforehand how the members of that group are alike. If you have a congregation to instruct and they range from little children to the very old, remember that in many ways they are all alike. In spite of age differences and in spite of all the other differences, in many ways they are similar. If you keep that in mind, you can teach them all. The Lord did.
>
> For example, take the expression "everyone loves a story," and you may see what I mean. If you have a point to put across and can illustrate it with a story, all can be taught. If you tell it in simple terms, a youngster can understand it; at the same time the oldest person may draw a great lesson from it. That is one of the reasons the Lord taught in parables. By so doing, He was teaching everybody at once, but not all of them the same lesson. (*Teach Ye Diligently*, pp. 102–3.)

Elder Mark E. Petersen wisely observed that "conversion is the ultimate goal of all teaching in the Church" ("The Power of Testimony," *Instructor*, August 1970, p. 273). When the rich experiences in the scriptures that tap into the values and principles of the gospel and radiate the inner workings of the Spirit are compared to similar, modern examples (as illustrated by the personal experiences of faithful Saints), a desire for growth towards perfection can be intensified and strengthened in those who read or hear them.

What is it that motivates someone to want to change, to be converted to true ideals, and to rededicate their lives to eternal values? Testimonies borne by those who are converted can play a significant motivating role in such a process. In this connection, it is interesting to note Joseph Smith's teaching that the ancient Saints' faith in God and their seeking a knowledge of his character were based, first of all, on the testimony of their fathers. "It was human testimony, and human testimony only," taught the Prophet, that motivated the ancients to seek after "a knowledge of the glory of God." (See *Lectures on Faith* 2:56.)

Elder Bruce R. McConkie explained the following approach to sharing faith-promoting stories: "Perhaps the perfect pattern in presenting faith-promoting stories is to teach what is found in the scriptures and then to put a seal of living reality upon it by telling a similar and equivalent thing that has happened in our dispensation and to our people and—most ideally—to us as individuals" ("The How and Why of Faith-promoting Stories," *New Era*, July 1978, p. 5).

This volume matches scriptural messages from the Old Testament with mostly contemporary stories that encourage the Saints to see, hear, and know the things of the Spirit for themselves in the same way Nephi, Abraham, and Joseph Smith did—by the power of the Holy Ghost. These experiences from the lives of ancient prophets and the parallels drawn from the lives of mostly modern people, the majority of them being Latter-day Saints, testify of the divinity of the scriptures and their Author, who is the same yesterday, today, and forever.

How to Tell a Story

Storytelling is an art. Although some teachers seem to be able to relate stories more easily than other teachers, it takes practice. A reminder of some of the basics of storytelling may help you more effectively use the great stories found in the scriptures and the modern parallels found in this book.

1. Select the story that best illustrates the gospel principle you are teaching. One excellent instructor, stake president Theron D. Rose, said, "Select a story that fits your topic and also fits you. A story *fits* you if it *hits* you— that is, it touches you, spiritually speaking."
2. Outline the story, including the facts, key thoughts, and essential phrases. This could be done mentally by underlining the important points while you read the story, or physically by creating an outline on paper.
3. Practice telling the story, using the outline as needed, until it flows smoothly and you are comfortable that no essential information has been left out.
4. When telling the story, don't embellish the facts. Avoid extremely sensational stories and hearsay. And if the story is one that is not in print, show respect for others' experiences by asking their permission prior to sharing it with others.
5. Tell the story with sincere gospel enthusiasm while keeping eye contact with your class or group. President Rose adds, "You may want to add facial expressions, appropriate gestures, voice intonation and fluctuation, and so on, as you desire. But, as a rule, just tell the story in your own sincere, enthusiastic way. Your students will love it! (And so will you!)"

He Whom God Calls, God Qualifies

Moses 6:26–47

As Enoch was journeying in the land among his people, "the Spirit of God descended out of heaven, and abode upon him. And he heard a voice from heaven, saying: Enoch, my son, prophesy unto this people, and say unto them—Repent, for thus saith the Lord: I am angry with this people, and my fierce anger is kindled against them; for their hearts have waxed hard, and their ears are dull of hearing, and their eyes cannot see afar off; . . . [they] have . . . gone astray, and have denied me, and have sought their own counsels in the dark . . . , and have not kept the commandments, which I gave unto their father, Adam."

When Enoch heard these words, he was humbled and bowed himself to the earth:

> Why is it that I have found favor in thy sight, and am but a lad, and all the people hate me; for I am slow of speech; wherefore am I thy servant?
>
> And the Lord said unto Enoch: Go forth and do as I have commanded thee, and no man shall pierce thee. Open thy mouth, and it shall be filled, and I will give thee utterance, for all flesh is in my hands, and I will do as seemeth me good.
>
> Say unto this people: Choose ye this day, to serve the Lord God who made you.

Behold my Spirit is upon you, wherefore all thy words will I justify; and the mountains shall flee before you, and the rivers shall turn from their course; and thou shalt abide in me, and I in you; therefore walk with me. . . .

And it came to pass that Enoch went forth in the land, among the people, standing upon the hills and the high places, and cried with a loud voice, testifying against their works; and all men were offended because of him.

And they came forth to hear him, upon the high places, saying unto the tent-keepers: Tarry ye here and keep the tents, while we go yonder to behold the seer, for he prophesieth, and there is a strange thing in the land; a wild man hath come among us.

And it came to pass when they heard him, no man laid hands on him; for fear came on all them that heard him; for he walked with God. . . .

And as Enoch spake forth the words of God, the people trembled, and could not stand in his presence. (Moses 6:26–28, 31–34, 37–39, 47.)

Rock of My Refuge

The first months of his mission in 1857 were not pleasant for Moses Thatcher. Just 15 years old, he had been a member of the Church for just four months when he was called to the ministry and assigned to labor with Elder Henry G. Boyle, the missionary who baptized him.

Not only did he have to wrestle with a terrible case of homesickness, he had a difficult time mastering missionary skills. His first speaking assignment was disastrous. "To undertake to preach to many who knew me as a rider of wild horses and a lassoer of wilder calves was a task for which I felt wholly unqualified," he said. "The very thought of attempting it made me ill. So when I tried, by request, to express gratitude for the restoration of the gospel, not a word could I utter."

To avoid any similar experiences, the boy pled with Elder Boyle not to call on him to pray or preach in public. "I said that if I could be excused from that, I would be Brother

Boyle's obedient and willing servant," Elder Thatcher said. "I said I would black his boots, wait on him, care for his horse and in every possible manner render myself useful to him, if only I didn't have to speak."

For several weeks, his appeals were mercifully regarded. But one Sunday, young Moses attended a Methodist church meeting without Elder Boyle. The minister viciously attacked the saints, lashing out particularly at Joseph Smith and Brigham Young. "Being the only one of the faith present, I was profoundly moved," Elder Thatcher said. "In humble, earnest inward prayer I besought the Lord to manifest to me my duty, and give me strength to perform it."

He was impressed to stand and reply to the minister's charges. "The Spirit of God came upon me, and powerfully, without the least hesitation or manifestation of timidity, I disproved many of the assertions of the vilifier," Elder Thatcher reported. He said he quoted scriptures that he had never read, the words and sentences appearing before his "spiritual eyes, as from an open book."

"I made the Lord the Rock of my refuge," Elder Thatcher said. "And thus did the Almighty with the weak confound the mighty, vindicate truth and unmistakably demonstrate that, however inadequate the instrument, He was able to make truth triumph over error." (Joseph Walker, " 'Rock of My Refuge,' " in "Missionary Moments" column, *Church News,* 7 August 1983, p. 16.)

We Will
Receive Them

Moses 7:60–64

The prophet Enoch was priviliged to see the last days in vision. The Lord described to him how "righteousness" would be showered down from heaven when He restored His church and kingdom to the earth. The Lord also told Enoch that He would send forth truth—that is, the Book of Mormon—"out of the earth, to bear testimony of mine Only Begotten; his resurrection from the dead; yea, and also the resurrection of all men; and righteousness and truth will I cause to sweep the earth as with a flood, to gather out mine elect from the four quarters of the earth." (Moses 7:62.)

Next the Lord described the Holy City, "called Zion, a New Jerusalem," that the Saints would build. He told Enoch of the great reunion the righteous will have in this heavenly city: "Then shalt thou and all thy city meet them there, and we will receive them into our bosom, and they shall see us; and we will fall upon their necks, and they shall fall upon our necks, and we will kiss each other; and there shall be mine abode, and it shall be Zion." (Moses 7:62–64.)

Jesus lived, and, as the Book of Mormon bears witness, he lives. When he entreats us to become like him, he does so in order that we might have his joy, the fulness of which we presently can only guess at. But a glorious rendezvous with the Lord awaits the righteous. At the "beckoning City of God," Elder Neal A. Maxwell observed, "the sole and self-assigned gatekeeper is

Jesus Christ" ("'True Believers in Christ,'" in *1980 Devotional Speeches of the Year: BYU Devotional and Fireside Addresses* [Provo, Utah: Brigham Young University Press, 1981], p. 139). As Nephi further testified, "the keeper of the gate is the Holy One of Israel; and he employeth no servant there; and there is none other way" (2 Nephi 9:41). The Lord loves us with a perfect love; he stands there "with open arms to receive [us]" (Mormon 6:17).

Elder Maxwell lovingly pleaded: "Do nothing to mar that moment. Do not allow yourselves to be deflected from that straight and narrow path, but seek to arrive at that rendezvous in such a circumstance, spiritually, that you can be drenched with joy and know the touch of those arms, for His arms of mercy and love are extended for you. I certify to you that that rendezvous is a reality. For some of you, it will come soon and some later, but it will come, if you are faithful. Of that, I testify!" (*The Education of Our Desires* [address delivered at the Salt Lake Institute of Religion, 5 January 1983], p. 11.)

A Beautiful Vision

On Tuesday, 10 May 1921, Elder David O. McKay and Brother Hugh J. Cannon were approaching Apia, Samoa. They had been sent by President Heber J. Grant to every mission and every stake around the world they could reach. Elder McKay recorded the following experience:

> We sailed all day on the smoothest sea of our entire trip. . . .
> Nearing Savaii, we could see with the aid of field glasses the "Spouting Horns," which looked like geysers. On our right we caught a glimpse of the little village nestling safely in the mouth of an extinct volcano on the little island of Apolima.
> Towards evening, the reflection of the afterglow of a beautiful sunset was most splendid! The sky was tinged with pink, and the clouds lingering around the horizon were fringed with various hues of crimson and orange, while the heavy cloud farther to the west was sombre purple and black.

These various colors cast varying shadows on the peaceful surface of the water. Those from the cloud were long and dark, those from the crimson-tinged sky, clear but rose-tinted and fading into a faint pink that merged into the clear blue of the ocean. Gradually, the shadows became deeper and heavier, and then all merged into a beautiful calm twilight that made the sea look like a great mirror upon which fell the faint light of the crescent moon!

Pondering still upon this beautiful scene, I lay in my berth at ten o'clock that night, and thought to myself: Charming as it is, it doesn't stir my soul with emotion as do the innocent lives of children, and the sublime characters of loved ones and friends. Their beauty, unselfishness, and heroism are after all the most glorious!

I then fell asleep, and beheld in vision something infinitely sublime. In the distance I beheld a beautiful white city. Though far away, yet I seemed to realize that trees with luscious fruit, shrubbery with gorgeously-tinted leaves, and flowers in perfect bloom abounded everywhere. The clear sky above seemed to reflect these beautiful shades of color. I then saw a great concourse of people approaching the city. Each one wore a white flowing robe, and a white headdress. Instantly my attention seemed centered upon their Leader, and though I could see only the profile of his features and his body, I recognized him at once as my Savior! The tint and radiance of his countenance were glorious to behold! There was a peace about him which seemed sublime—it was divine!

The city, I understood, was his. It was the City Eternal; and the people following him were to abide there in peace and eternal happiness.

But who were they?

As if the Savior read my thoughts, he answered by pointing to a semicircle that then appeared above them, and on which were written in gold the words:

"These Are They Who Have Overcome the World—
Who Have Truly Been Born Again!"

When I awoke, it was breaking day over Apia harbor. (*Cherished Experiences from the Writings of President David O. McKay*, comp. Clare Middlemiss [Salt Lake City: Deseret Book Co., 1955], pp. 108–9.)

Gratitude

Genesis 14:20

The Lord called Abraham to leave his homeland in Ur (near the Persian Gulf in present-day Iraq) and travel with his family toward a new, promised land (see Abraham 1:16). He was first led to Haran (see Genesis 11:31), an important trading center near the source of the Euphrates River. The Lord appeared to Abraham at Haran and made a covenant with him, promising all gospel blessings to Abraham and his seed and through his descendants to all the world (see Genesis 12:2–3; Abraham 2:7–12), and directed Abraham to leave Haran for the promised land of Israel (see Abraham 2:6; Genesis 12:1, 4).

Abraham took his wife, Sarai, and Lot, his nephew, and "the souls that [they] had won in Haran" (Abraham 2:15) and went to the land of Canaan (modern-day Israel). Abraham discovered an idolatrous nation living there, so he offered sacrifice and prayed for help. The Lord appeared to Abraham and declared, "Unto thy seed will I give this land" (Abraham 2:19; Genesis 12:7). Because of a grievous famine in Canaan, the Lord led Abraham to Egypt. There he was invited to sit on Pharaoh's throne and teach the principles of astronomy, and presumably he also taught the Egyptians the eternal plan of salvation that he had been taught by the Lord. (See Genesis 12:10–20; Abraham 2:21–25; 3.)

After fulfilling his mission to Egypt, Abraham returned to Canaan. He had been blessed with great wealth by the Lord—he

"was very rich in cattle, in silver, and in gold" (Genesis 13:2)—
but he was humble and a man of great faith and righteousness.
His Christlike nature was revealed when he graciously allowed
Lot to choose where to live, either in the well-watered plain of
Jordan, which was as beautiful "as the garden of the Lord," or in
the desert climate of Canaan (see Genesis 13:5–11). Because
Abraham was the patriarch, Lot, who had been cared for and
protected by Abraham, should have insisted that Abraham
choose first. Abraham's only concern was that "there be no
strife" between them, so he let Lot make the first choice (see
Genesis 13:8–9). Lot chose the plain of Jordan and pitched his
tent "toward Sodom" and Gomorrah (Genesis 13:12).

A fierce battle erupted between the rival kings of the neighboring city-states, and Lot was taken captive along with many
from Sodom and Gomorrah (see Genesis 14:1–12). When
Abraham learned what had happened, he immediately "armed
his trained servants" and battled for Lot's safety. Abraham's band
of servants routed the mob, saving Lot's life and family and
recovering all Lot's possessions. (See Genesis 14:13–16.)

Returning home, Abraham met the great high priest
Melchizedek, the patriarch whose name means "king of righteousness" and to whom the honor has gone of having the Holy
Priesthood after the Order of the Son of God named after him
(see D&C 107:2–4). Melchizedek blessed Abraham and prayed
in gratitude to the Lord for safely delivering him from Lot's enemies: "Blessed be the most high God, which hath delivered thine
enemies into thy hand." And Abraham paid him tithes of all he
possessed. (See Genesis 14:18–20).

Then Abraham met the king of Sodom, who desired to
reward Abraham for saving his people as well as Lot. "Give me
the persons, and take the goods to thyself," the king said. "And
Abram said to the king of Sodom, I have lift up mine hand unto
the Lord, the most high God, the possessor of heaven and earth,
That I will not take from a thread even to a shoelatchet, and
that I will not take any thing that is thine, lest thou shouldest
say, I have made Abram rich." (Genesis 14:21–23.)

President Spencer W. Kimball commented on the humility

of Abraham, "The king of Sodom knew nothing about Abraham's covenant with the Lord; Abraham could have made himself rich by receiving of the king's generosity. But he had made an oath which he would not violate. Oh, that all of God's children could be so true!" ("The Example of Abraham," *Ensign*, June 1975, p. 6.)

Abraham's entire life provides an example of a man who was greatly blessed by the Lord but who never failed to show gratitude for the blessings he had received.

The Parable of the Grateful Cat

Sometimes we forget how much the Lord has really done for us. Like Abraham, we too should feel an overwhelming sense of gratitude for the Lord's goodness to us. Our hearts should be full of such gratitude for what the Savior did in Gethsemane and in his glorious resurrection, as well as for the blessings God sends us daily to sustain us. We can all sense that it was out of love for us that the Savior knelt in Gethsemane and that the Father allowed his Son to suffer (see John 3:16; D&C 34:1, 3). What can we do to repay them for their love?

Elder James E. Talmage told of a naturalist in the nineteenth century who, in the course of his customary daily walk, left his cottage and came to a millpond. At the edge of the water he saw two boys with a basket. In the basket were three whining kittens, and a mother cat paced frantically back and forth on the shore as two other kittens were drowning in the water.

Upset with what he was witnessing, the scientist's inquiries elicited the fact that the boys were servants to a wealthy family. The mistress of the great estate had this old mother cat which she loved, but didn't want any more cats around. When the mother cat delivered kittens, the woman told the two boys to drown them.

The naturalist gave the boys a shilling apiece, saying he would make sure the boys wouldn't get in trouble if they would let him take the remaining three kittens (death had already claimed the two in the water). Much to the man's surprise, it was as though the mother cat understood exactly what was happening. Elder Talmage's account continues:

> The mother cat evinced more than the measure of intelligence usually attributed to the animal world. She recognized the man as the deliverer of her three children, who but for him would have been drowned. As he carried the kittens she trotted along—sometimes following, sometimes alongside, occasionally rubbing against him with grateful yet mournful purrs. At his home [he] provided the kittens with comfortable quarters, and left the mother cat in joyful content. She seemed to have forgotten the death of the two in her joy over the rescue of the three.
>
> Next day, the gentleman was seated in his parlor on the ground floor, in the midst of a notable company. Many people had gathered to do honor to the distinguished naturalist. The cat came in. In her mouth she carried a large, fat mouse, not dead, but still feebly struggling under the pains of torturous capture. She laid her panting and well-nigh expiring prey at the feet of the man who had saved her kittens.

Then Elder Talmage drew a marvelous lesson of gratitude from this story:

> What think you of the offering, and of the purpose that prompted the act? A live mouse, fleshy and fat! Within the cat's power of possible estimation and judgment it was a superlative gift. To her limited understanding no rational creature could feel otherwise than pleased over the present of a meaty mouse. Every sensible cat would be ravenously joyful with such an offering. Beings unable to appreciate a mouse for a meal were unknown to the cat.
>
> Are not our offerings to the Lord—our tithes and our other free-will gifts—as thoroughly unnecessary to His needs as was the mouse to the scientist? But remember that the grateful and sacrificing nature of the cat was enlarged, and in a measure sanctified, by her offering.
>
> Thanks be to God that He gages the offerings and sacri-

fices of His children by the standard of their physical ability and honest intent rather than by the gradation of His exalted station. Verily He is God with us; and He both understands and accepts our motives and righteous desires. Our need to serve God is incalculably greater than His need for our service. ("The Parable of the Grateful Cat," *Improvement Era*, August 1916, pp. 875–76.)

Trials Often Precede
Great Blessings

Genesis 15:12, 17–18

The Lord appeared to father Abraham at Haran and in effect promised him an eternal marriage to Sarah; also, a righteous posterity (in number "as the stars of the heaven," Genesis 22:17), that all gospel blessings would come to his descendants and from them to all mankind, and that his family would receive a land inheritance in Israel (see Genesis 15:1–11; Abraham 2:8–11). But before the blessing and covenant were bestowed, there were trials to be endured. "And when the sun was going down, a deep sleep fell upon Abram; and, lo, an horror of great darkness fell upon him. . . . And it came to pass. . . . in the same day the Lord made a covenant with Abram." (Genesis 15:12, 17–18.)

Modern prophets have reported similar trials.

The Prophet Joseph Smith

In 1838 the Prophet Joseph Smith dictated an account of events from his life and from the early history of the Church. Excerpts from that account now appear in the Pearl of Great Price, from which is taken the following recital of the Prophet's quest to find out which church to join:

While I was laboring under the extreme difficulties

caused by the contests of these parties of religionists, I was one day reading the Epistle of James, first chapter and fifth verse, which reads: *If any of you lack wisdom, let him ask of God, that giveth to all men liberally, and upbraideth not; and it shall be given him. . . .*

At length I came to the conclusion that I must either remain in darkness and confusion, or else I must do as James directs, that is, ask of God. I at length came to the determination to "ask of God," concluding that if he gave wisdom to them that lacked wisdom, and would give liberally, and not upbraid, I might venture.

So, in accordance with this, my determination to ask of God, I retired to the woods to make the attempt. It was on the morning of a beautiful, clear day, early in the spring of eighteen hundred and twenty. It was the first time in my life that I had made such an attempt, for amidst all my anxieties I had never as yet made the attempt to pray vocally.

After I had retired to the place where I had previously designed to go, having looked around me, and finding myself alone, I kneeled down and began to offer up the desires of my heart to God. I had scarcely done so, when immediately I was seized upon by some power which entirely overcame me, and had such an astonishing influence over me as to bind my tongue so that I could not speak. Thick darkness gathered around me, and it seemed to me for a time as if I were doomed to sudden destruction. (Joseph Smith—History 1:11, 13–15.)

In another account of these events (given in 1835), the Prophet described this encounter with the powers of darkness in these terms: "My tongue seemed to be swollen in my mouth, so that I could not utter. I heard a noise behind me like some one walking towards me: I strove again to pray, but could not; the noise of walking seemed to draw nearer; I sprang upon my feet and looked round, but saw no person, or thing that was calculated to produce the noise of walking." (*The Papers of Joseph Smith*, ed. Dean C. Jessee, vol. 1, *Autobiographical and Historical Writings* [Salt Lake City: Deseret Book Co., 1989], p. 127, spelling standardized.)

The Prophet's 1838 account continues:

> But, exerting all my powers to call upon God to deliver
> me out of the power of this enemy which had seized upon
> me, and at the very moment when I was ready to sink into
> despair and abandon myself to destruction—not to an imagi-
> nary ruin, but to the power of some actual being from the
> unseen world, who had such marvelous power as I had never
> before felt in any being—just at this moment of great alarm, I
> saw a pillar of light exactly over my head, above the bright-
> ness of the sun, which descended gradually until it fell upon
> me.
>   It no sooner appeared than I found myself delivered from
> the enemy which held me bound. When the light rested
> upon me I saw two Personages, whose brightness and glory
> defy all description, standing above me in the air. One of
> them spake unto me, calling me by name and said, pointing
> to the other—*This is My Beloved Son. Hear Him!* (Joseph
> Smith—History 1:16–17.)

Hugh B. Brown's Call to Be a General Authority

Hugh B. Brown was called to be an Assistant to the Quorum
of the Twelve in 1953, to be a member of the Quorum of the
Twelve in 1958, and to be a member of the First Presidency in
1961. In the following excerpt from a 1964 address to the
Church College of Hawaii student body, President Brown
recounts his experiences around the time of his call to be a
General Authority:

> I think I should not leave you this morning without
> bearing my testimony to you. I have no object in deceiving
> you. There is nothing to be gained by lying to you, and what
> I shall now say comes from the very center of my heart. It has
> to do with my convictions—convictions gained over a period
> of sixty to eighty years, convictions regarding myself, my
> sources, my destiny, my God and my relationship to him. I
> can say to you my young friends, that God has been so good

to me as to give me an individual testimony of the divinity of his son, Jesus Christ. He is, in fact, the Son of the living God, the Redeemer of the world, its Savior. I know that to be true. I know it as I know of few other things in the world. May I just take a moment of your time to give you one incident to illustrate how I know it. This is a little unknown chapter out of my own life. It illustrates how I know that God lives.

We were in Canada. I was, as has been noted by Brother Cook, an attorney for an oil company and a manager of it. We were drilling wells and making money. I was at the moment up in the Canadian Rockies way back from the highways. We were drilling there. Everything looked very prosperous. I woke very early one morning before daylight. I was troubled in my mind and I didn't know the source or the reason for the trouble. And I began to pray, but didn't seem to get an answer. And I remembered that the Savior was wont to go into the mountain tops frequently. You remember, his life was punctuated by mountain peaks. There is the mountain peak of the temptation, there is the mountain peak of the transfiguration, there is the mountain peak of the Beatitudes, there is the mountain peak from which he took flight into heaven. So thinking about this, I arose before daylight and went back up into the hills where I knew no one would be near. And when I got up on an advantageous point, I began to talk out loud. I was talking to God! Now, I do not mean that he was standing there listening to me or replying to me. But I mean from the very center of my heart I was calling to Him.

Now my family were all in good health, all quite prosperous, and it looked as for myself that within a few days I would be a multimillionaire. And yet, I was troubled. And up there on that mountain peak I said to Him, "O God, if what it seems is about to happen will happen, and if it is not to be for the best good of myself and my family and my friends, don't let it happen. Take it from me." (May I just pause here and say to you young fellows, don't you make that kind of a proposition to the Lord, because He's liable to take you up on it. He did me!) I said, "Don't let it happen unless in your wisdom it is good for me." Well, I left the mountains and came down to the camp. I got into my car and drove to the city of

Edmonton. It was a Friday and while I was driving I was thinking of what had happened. And I felt that there was something impending that I couldn't understand. When I arrived home, and after a bite to eat, I said to Sister Brown, "I think I'll occupy the back bedroom because I'm afraid I'm not going to sleep." Now I went in there alone and there, through the night, I had the most terrible battle with the powers of the adversary. I wanted to destroy myself. Not in the sense of suicide, but something within me was impelling me to wish that I could cease to be and be rubbed out. It was terrific. The blackness was so thick you could feel it.

Sister Brown came in later in the night, toward morning in fact, wanting to know what was the matter. And when she closed the door, she said, "What's in this room?" And I said, "Nothing but the power of the devil is in this room." And we knelt together by the bedside and prayed for release. We spent the night together, the balance of it. And in the morning I went down to my office. It was Saturday now and there was no one at the office. And in going into the office, I knelt by a cot and asked God for deliverance from the darkness that had enveloped me. And coming from somewhere there was an element of peace, the kind of peace that rests on the souls of men when they make contact with God. And I called her and said, "Everything is all right, or is going to be!"

That night at 10:00 o'clock, October 1953—the telephone rang. Sister Brown answered. She called me and said, "Salt Lake's calling," and I wondered who could be calling me from that far away. I took the phone and said, "Hello." "This is David O. McKay calling. The Lord wants you to give the balance of your life to Him and His Church. We are in a conference of the Church. The concluding session will be tomorrow afternoon. Can you get here?"

I couldn't get there because there were no planes flying. I told him I couldn't come. I didn't ask him how much he would give me if I gave up the good job I had. But I did decide to go. I knew that a call had come. And the call came after this awful conflict with the adversary. And when he said, "I want you to give the balance of your life to the Church," I knew that it meant giving up the money. It meant that I'd turn over everything to someone else and go to Salt Lake without monetary remuneration.

Since that time, I've been happier than ever before in my life. The men with whom I was associated have made millions. And yet, when one of them was in my office not long ago in Salt Lake, he said, "I am worth at least seven million dollars. I would gladly give every dollar of it to you if you could give me what you have. I can't buy it with money, but I'd like to have what you have. What you have is peace of soul and I cannot buy that with money."

. . . I pray that God will be with you and inspire you individually and collectively that you may live up to your opportunities and be worthy of your source and your potential destiny. I pray that the Spirit of the Lord may . . . remain with you when you return to your homes that you may inspire others to greater efforts, to higher ideals, to living the Gospel of Jesus Christ. (*Eternal Progression* [address delivered at the Church College of Hawaii, 16 October 1964], pp. 8–10.)

Wrestling for a Blessing

Genesis 32:24–28

One night the patriarch Jacob wrestled for a blessing from the Lord until the breaking of the day. He prevailed and thus was named "Israel." (See Genesis 32:24–28.)

A Modern Prophet Wrestles for a Blessing

About three months following his call to the Quorum of the Twelve, Elder Spencer W. Kimball said in general conference:

I believe the brethren were very kind to me in announcing my appointment when they did so that I might make the necessary adjustments in my business affairs, but perhaps they were more inspired to give me the time that I needed of a long period of purification, for in those long days and weeks I did a great deal of thinking and praying, and fasting and praying. There were conflicting thoughts that surged through my mind—seeming voices saying: "You can't do the work. You are not worthy. You have not the ability"—and always finally came the triumphant thought: "You must do the work assigned—you must make yourself able, worthy and qualified." And the battle raged on.

I remember reading that Jacob wrestled all night, "until the breaking of the day," for a blesssing; and I want to tell you that for eighty-five nights I have gone through that experience, wrestling for a blessing. Eighty-five times, the breaking of the day has found me on my knees praying to the Lord to help me and strengthen me and make me equal to this great responsibility that has come to me. (In Conference Report, October 1943, pp. 15–16.)

Wrestling with Joseph and Receiving a Blessing

Howard Coray was born on 6 May 1817. Frontier life was hard, but especially for one as small as Howard Coray. He was born with his left arm shorter than his right arm, the left arm extending only about two inches below the elbow. His parents moved their family to Pennsylvania about 1830. And in March of 1840 he joined the Church, being baptized by Joseph Wood. He moved to Nauvoo, where he met and worked for the Prophet Joseph Smith, serving as his secretary for quite some time. He recorded an experience he had with the Prophet Joseph (for readability, paragraph breaks have been introduced below that don't occur in the original source):

I met with an accident which I shall here mention: The Prophet and myself, after looking at his horses, and admiring them, that were just across the road from his house, we started thither. The Prophet at this time put his arm over my shoulder. When we had reached about the middle of the road, he stopped and remarked: "Brother Coray, I wish you was a little larger. I would like to have some fun with you."

I replied, "Perhaps you can as it is"—not realizing what I was saying. Joseph a man of over 200 pounds weight, while I scarcely 130 pounds, made it not a little ridiculous for me to think of engaging with him in anything like a scuffle.

However, as soon as I made this reply, he began to trip me. He took some kind of a lock on my right leg, from which I was unable to extricate it; and throwing me around, broke it some three inches above the ankle joint.

He immediately carried me into the house, pulled off my boot, and found at once that my leg was decidedly broken;

then got some splinters and bandaged it. A number of times that day did he come in to see me, endeavoring to console me as much as possible.

The next day when he happened in to see me, after a little conversation I said: "Brother Joseph, when Jacob wrestled with the angel and was lamed by him, the angel blessed him. Now I think I am also entitled to a blessing."

To this he replied: "I am not the Patriarch, but my father is, and when you get up and around, I'll have him bless you."

He said no more for a minute or so, meanwhile looking very earnestly at me; then said, "Brother Coray, you will soon find a companion, one that will be suited to your condition, and whom you will be satisfied with. She will cling to you like the cords of death; and you will have a good many children." He also said some other things, which I can't so distinctly remember. . . .

Subsequent, some three or four weeks, to getting my leg broke, and while at meeting, the blessing of the Prophet came into my mind, viz: that I should soon find a companion, etc., etc. So I thought I would take a square look at the congregation and see who there was, that possibly the fair one promised me might be present. After looking and gazing a while at the audience, my eyes settled upon a young lady sitting in a one-horse buggy. She was an entire stranger to me, and a resident of some other place. . . .

She had dark brown eyes, very bright and penetrating (at least they penetrated me), and I said to myself, "She will do."

The fact is, I was decidedly struck. After the dismissal of the meeting, instead of going for my dinner I remained on the ground and presently commenced promenading about to see what I could see. I had not gone far before I came square in front of the lovely miss, walking arm in arm with a Mrs. Harris, whom I was well acquainted with. They stopped and Mrs. Harris said, "Brother Coray, I have the honor of introducing you to Miss Martha Knowlton, from Bear Creek."

I, of course, bowed as politely as I knew how, and she curtsied, and we then fell into somewhat familiar conversation. I discovered at once that she was ready, offhand, and inclined to be witty; also, that her mind took a wider range than was common for young ladies of her age.

This interview, though short, was indeed very enjoyable, and closed with the hope that she might be the one whom the Lord had picked for me. And thus it proved to be.

I shall not go into all the details of our courtship; suffice it to say, every move I made seemed to count one in the right direction. I let Brother Joseph into the secret—showed him a letter that I had written, designed for her. He seemed to take uncommon interest in the matter, took pains to see her and talk with her about me, telling her that I was just the one for her. A few letters passed between us. I visited her at her home, proposed, was accepted; and on the 6th day of February 1841 we were married at her father's house, Brother Robert B. Thompson performing the ceremony. (Journal of Howard Coray, Archives Division, Church Historical Department, The Church of Jesus Christ of Latter-day Saints, Salt Lake City, Utah, pp. 8–11, spelling and punctuation standardized. See also Hyrum L. Andrus and Helen Mae Andrus, *They Knew the Prophet* [Salt Lake City: Bookcraft, 1974], pp. 135–37.)

Not only did Howard Coray and Martha Knowlton marry, but they raised a large family of twelve children and eventually came west with the Saints. Before leaving Nauvoo they met with Lucy Mack Smith and encouraged her to write the history of her family, including the early life of the Prophet Joseph. Thanks to their efforts, we now have *History of Joseph Smith by His Mother*. In addition, Martha became one of the first women in America to be invited to sit on a board of a major university, Brigham Young Academy.

How Can I Do This Great Wickedness, and Sin Against God?

Genesis 39:1–23

And Joseph was brought down to Egypt; and Potiphar, an officer of Pharaoh, captain of the guard, an Egyptian, bought him of the hands of the Ishmeelites, which had brought him down thither. . . .

And his master saw that the Lord was with him, and that the Lord made all that he did to prosper in his hand.

And Joseph found grace in his sight, and he served him. . . .

And it came to pass from the time that he had made him overseer in his house, and over all that he had, that the Lord blessed the Egyptian's house for Joseph's sake; and the blessing of the Lord was upon all that he had in the house, and in the field.

And he left all that he had in Joseph's hand; and he knew not ought he had, save the bread which he did eat. And Joseph was a goodly person, and well favoured.

And it came to pass after these things, that his master's wife cast her eyes upon Joseph; and she said, Lie with me.

But he refused, and said unto his master's wife, Behold, my master wotteth not what is with me in the house, and he hath committed all that he hath to my hand;

There is none greater in this house than I; neither hath he kept back any thing from me but thee, because thou art his wife: how then can I do this great wickedness, and sin against God?

And it came to pass, as she spake to Joseph day by day, that he hearkened not unto her, to lie by her, or to be with her.

And it came to pass about this time, that Joseph went into the house to do his business; and there was none of the men of the house there within.

And she caught him by his garment, saying, Lie with me: and he left his garment in her hand, and fled, and got him out.

And it came to pass, when she saw that he had left his garment in her hand, and was fled forth,

That she called unto the men of her house, and spake unto them, saying, See, he hath brought in an Hebrew unto us to mock us; he came in unto me to lie with me, and I cried with a loud voice:

And it came to pass, when he heard that I lifted up my voice and cried, that he left his garment with me, and fled, and got him out.

And she laid up his garment by her, until his lord came home.

And she spake unto him according to these words, saying, The Hebrew servant, which thou has brought unto us, came in unto me to mock me:

And it came to pass, as I lifted up my voice and cried, that he left his garment with me, and fled out.

And it came to pass, when his master heard the words of his wife, which she spake unto him, saying, After this manner did thy servant to me; that his wrath was kindled.

And Joseph's master took him, and put him into the prison, a place where the king's prisoners were bound: and he was there in the prison.

But the Lord was with Joseph, and shewed him mercy, and gave him favour in the sight of the keeper of the prison.

And the keeper of the prison committed to Joseph's hand all the prisoners that were in the prison; and whatsoever they did there, he was the doer of it.

The keeper of the prison looked not to any thing that was under his hand; because the Lord was with him, and that which he did, the Lord made it to prosper. (Genesis 39:1, 3–23.)

Susanna and the Judgment of Daniel

The Apocrypha contains some of the sacred writings of the Jewish people which were not included in the Hebrew Bible. These writings help form a valuable connection between the Old and New Testaments. (See LDS Bible Dictionary, s.v. "Apocrypha," p. 610.) With regard to the Apocrypha, the Prophet Joseph Smith learned by revelation that "there are many things contained therein that are true, and it is mostly translated correctly"; but that "there are many things contained therein that are not true, which are interpolations by the hands of men. . . . Therefore, whoso readeth it, let him understand, for the Spirit manifesteth truth; and whoso is enlightened by the Spirit shall obtain benefit therefrom." (D&C 91:1–2, 4–5.)

One of the great stories in the Apocrypha is about Susanna, a faithful and virtuous woman. Her example of courage and trust in the Lord is worthy of emulation. Her experience also introduces us to Daniel, the Old Testament prophet.

In Babylon there lived a man named Joakim. He had married Susanna daughter of Hilkiah, a woman of great beauty; and she was God-fearing, because her parents were worthy people and had instructed their daughter in the Law of Moses. Joakim was a very rich man, and had a garden attached to his house; the Jews would often visit him since he was held in greater respect than any other man. Two elderly men had been selected from the people that year to act as judges. Of such the Lord said, "Wickedness has come to Babylon through the elders and judges posing as guides to the people." These men were often at Joakim's house, and all who were engaged in litigation used to come to them. At midday, when everyone had gone, Susanna used to take a walk in her husband's garden. The two elders, who used to watch her every day as she came in to take her walk, gradually began to desire her. They threw reason aside, making no effort to turn their eyes to heaven, and forgetting its demands of virtue. Both were inflamed by the same passion, but they hid their desire from each other, for they were ashamed to admit the longing to sleep with her, but they still contrived to see her every day. One day, having parted with the words, "Let us go home, it is time for the midday meal," they went off in different directions, only to retrace their steps and find themselves face to face again. Obliged then to explain, they admitted their desire and agreed to look for an opportunity of surprising her alone. So they waited for a favourable moment; and one day Susanna came as usual, accompanied only by two young maidservants. The day was hot and she wanted to bathe in the garden. There was no one about except the two elders, spying on her from their hiding place. She said to the servants, "Bring me some oil and balsam and shut the garden door while I bathe." They did as they were told, shutting the garden door and going back to the house by a side entrance to fetch what she had asked for; they knew nothing about the elders, who were hiding.

Hardly were the servants gone than the two elders were there after her. "Look," they said, "the garden door is shut, no one can see us. We want to have you, so give in and let us! Refuse, and we will both give evidence that a young man was with you and that was why you sent your maids away." Susanna sighed. "I am trapped," she said, "whatever I do. If I agree, that means my death; if I resist, I cannot get away from you. But I prefer to fall innocent into your power than to sin in the eyes of the Lord." Then she cried out as loud as she could. The two elders began shouting too, putting the blame on her, and one of them ran to open the garden door. The household, hearing the shouting in the garden, rushed out by the side entrance to see what was happening; once the elders had told their story the servants were thoroughly taken aback, since nothing of this sort had ever been said of Susanna.

Next day a meeting was held at the house of her husband Joakim. The two elders arrived, in their vindictiveness determined to have her put to death. They addressed the company: "Summon Susanna daughter of Hilkiah and wife of Joakim." She was sent for, and came accompanied by her parents, her children and all her relations. Susanna was very graceful and beautiful to look at; she was veiled, so the wretches made her unveil in order to feast their eyes on her beauty. All her own people were weeping, and so were all the others who saw her. The two elders stood up, with all the people round them, and laid their hands on the woman's head [the formal preliminary to death by stoning]. Tearfully she turned her eyes to heaven, her heart confident in God. The elders then spoke. "While we were walking by ourselves in the garden, this woman arrived with two servants. She shut the garden door and then dismissed the servants. A young man who had been hiding went over to her and they lay down together. From the end of the garden where we were, we saw this crime taking place and hurried towards them. Though we saw them together we were unable to catch the man: he was too strong for us; he opened the door and took to his heels. We did, however, catch this woman and ask her who the young man was. She refused to tell us. That is our evidence."

Since they were elders of the people, and judges, the assembly took their word: Susanna was condemned to death. She cried out as loud as she could, "Eternal God, you know all secrets and everything before it happens; you know that they have given false evidence against me. And now I have to die, innocent as I am of everything their malice has invented against me?"

The Lord heard her cry and, as she was being led away to die, he roused the holy spirit residing in a young boy named Daniel who began to shout, "I am innocent of this woman's death!" At which all the people turned to him and asked, "What do you mean by these words?" Standing in the middle of the crowd he replied, "Are you so stupid, sons of Israel, as to condemn a daughter of Israel unheard, and without troubling to find out the truth? Go back to the scene of the trial: these men have given false evidence against her."

All the people hurried back, and the elders said to Daniel, "Come and sit with us and tell us what you mean, since God has given you the gifts that elders have." Daniel said, "Keep the men well apart from each other for I want to question them." When the men had been separated, Daniel had one of them brought to him. "You have grown old in wickedness," he said, "and now the sins of your earlier days have overtaken you, you with your unjust judgements, your condemnation of the innocent, your acquittal of guilty men, when the Lord has said, 'You must not put the innocent and the just to death.' Now then, since you saw her so clearly, tell me what tree you saw them lying under?" He replied, "Under a mastic tree." Daniel said, "True enough! Your lie recoils on your own head: the angel of God has already received your sentence from him and will slash you in half." He dismissed the man, ordered the other to be brought and said to him, "Spawn of Canaan, not of Judah, beauty has seduced you, lust has led your heart astray! This is how you have been behaving with the daughters of Israel and they were too frightened to resist; but here is a daughter of Judah who could not stomach your wickedness! Now then, tell me what tree you surprised them under?" He replied, "Under a holm oak." Daniel said, "True enough! Your lie recoils on your own head: the angel of God is waiting, with a sword to drive home and split you, and destroy the pair of you."

Then the whole assembly shouted, blessing God, the saviour of those who trust in him. And they turned on the two elders whom Daniel had convicted of false evidence out of their own mouths. As prescribed in the Law of Moses, they sentenced them to the same punishment as they had intended to inflict on their neighbour. They put them to death; the life of an innocent woman was spared that day. Hilkiah and his wife gave thanks to God for their daughter Susanna, and so did her husband Joakim and all his relations, because she had been acquitted of anything dishonourable.

From that day onwards Daniel's reputation stood high with the people. (Daniel 13, Jerusalem Bible.)

The Lord Protected Israel

Exodus 14:19–23, 26–31

And the angel of God, which went before the camp of Israel, removed and went behind them; and the pillar of the cloud went from before their face, and stood behind them:

And it came between the camp of the Egyptians and the camp of Israel; and it was a cloud and darkness to them, but it gave light by night to these: so that the one came not near the other all the night.

And Moses stretched out his hand over the sea; and the Lord caused the sea to go back by a strong east wind all that night, and made the sea dry land, and the waters were divided.

And the children of Israel went into the midst of the sea upon the dry ground: and the waters were a wall unto them on their right hand, and on their left.

And the Egyptians pursued, and went in after them to the midst of the sea, even all Pharaoh's horses, his chariots, and his horsemen. . . .

And the Lord said unto Moses, Stretch out thine hand over the sea, that the waters may come again upon the Egyptians, upon their chariots, and upon their horsemen.

And Moses stretched forth his hand over the sea, and the sea returned to his strength when the morning appeared; and the Egyptians fled against it; and the Lord overthrew the Egyptians in the midst of the sea.

And the waters returned, and covered the chariots, and

the horsemen, and all the host of Pharaoh that came into the sea after them; there remained not so much as one of them.

But the children of Israel walked upon dry land in the midst of the sea; and the waters were a wall unto them on their right hand, and on their left.

Thus the Lord saved Israel that day out of the hand of the Egyptians; and Israel saw the Egyptians dead upon the sea shore.

And Israel saw that great work which the Lord did upon the Egyptians: and the people feared the Lord, and believed the Lord, and his servant Moses. (Exodus 14:19–23, 26–31.)

The Lord Protected Zion's Camp

In the summer of 1833, the Saints in Jackson County, Missouri, were being harassed by their enemies. A secret constitution was signed by many of the "old settlers" demanding that the Mormons leave the county. In the fall, Mormons were whipped and beaten, were driven from their homes, and had their property stolen or destroyed. In February 1834 the Prophet Joseph, living in Kirtland, Ohio, called the high council together and proposed to lead an army of brethren to restore the Saints to their property in Jackson County. Zion's Camp departed for Missouri in May. Eventually 207 men joined the march. They suffered much from fatigue, heat, humidity, and lack of food and water. Some days they walked as many as forty miles without adequate provisions. Yet most of these Saints were motivated by charity for their afflicted brothers and sisters and by a deep desire to see the Church in Jackson County rescued.

When news that the Mormon army was headed for Missouri reached Jackson County, several meetings were held by the old settlers. A meeting was called in Ray County, where almost a thousand people gathered. A delegation of Jackson County residents, headed by Samuel C. Owens, presented the demands of the people to some representatives of the Church, demands which the Mormons would find impossible to meet. Owens delivered an inflammatory speech against the Saints. A man named Riley said, "They must either clear out, or be cleared out."

The Jackson County delegation, led by Samuel Owens and James Campbell, started for the city of Independence, swearing they would raise an army large enough to annihilate the Mormon army before the latter ever reached Jackson County. Campbell vowed, while adjusting his pistols, "The eagles and turkey buzzards shall eat my flesh if I do not fix Joe Smith and his army so that their skins will not hold shucks, before two days are passed." (*History of the Church* 2:96–99.)

Drawing upon information from Joseph Smith's history and a discourse by Elder George A. Smith, historian Ivan J. Barrett describes what happened next:

> [Owens] and his companions went to the ferry and started across the river about dusk. While in midstream the ferry sprung a leak and began to sink. Joseph Smith in his history declared that "the angel of God saw fit to sink the boat about the middle of the river." When they discovered the boat was sinking Sam Owens shouted, "We must strip to the bone, or we shall all perish." But Campbell refused. "I will go to hell before I will land naked," he said. He had his choice and went to the bottom. Seven of the twelve were drowned. The body of Campbell floated downstream "some four or five miles, and lodged upon a pile of drift wood, where the eagles, buzzards, ravens, crows, and wild animals ate his flesh from his bones, to fulfill his own words, and left him a horrible example of God's vengeance." About three weeks later the bleaching bones which once held together his carcass were found by a Mr. Purtle.
>
> Owens stripped himself of every article of clothing and floated down the river. After making several attempts he finally reached the Jackson side of the river fourteen miles downstream from the ferry landing. Completely exhausted, he rested himself in the nettles which grew thick and to a great height on the Missouri bottoms. Walking through the high, profuse growth of nettles was Sam Owens's only possible chance of reaching the settlements. After walking four miles he came to the road and saw a young lady, the belle of

Jackson County, approaching on horseback. In his miserable condition he hid behind a log so she could not see him. When she rode up he called from his hiding place, "Madam, I am Samuel C. Owens, the Commander-in-Chief of the mob against the Mormons; I wish you to send some men from the next house with clothing, for I am naked." The belle of Jackson County dismounted and left him "a light shawl and a certain unmentionable under garment, and passed on. So," concluded George A. Smith, the narrator of this amusing incident, "His Excellency Samuel C. Owens, who was afterwards killed in Mexico by foolishly exposing himself, contrary to orders, took up his line of march for the town, in the shawl and petticoat uniform, after his expedition against the 'Mormons.'" ("Joseph Smith and the Restoration" [Ph.D. diss., Brigham Young University, 1967], p. 209. George A. Smith's talk is found in *Journal of Discourses* 2:22–24.)

The Parting of the Red Sea

Exodus 14:21–30

"And Moses stretched out his hand over the sea; and the Lord caused the sea to go back by a strong east wind all that night, and made the sea dry land, and the waters were divided. And the children of Israel went into the midst of the sea upon the dry ground: and the waters were a wall unto them on their right hand, and on their left. . . . The children of Israel walked upon dry land in the midst of the sea. . . . Thus the Lord saved Israel that day out of the hand of the Egyptians." (Exodus 14:21–22, 29–30.)

The Parting of the Ice

In February or March of 1831, Lucy Mack Smith and about eighty Saints hired a flatboat to take them down the Erie Canal to Buffalo, New York, where they would continue on to Kirtland and join the Prophet Joseph Smith. Lucy Mack Smith recorded their experience:

The people of the surrounding country came and bade us farewell, invoking the blessing of heaven upon our heads. . . .
. . . Soon after this, we were pushed off and under fine headway.

I then called the brethren and sisters together, and reminded them that we were traveling by the commandment of the Lord. . . . I then desired them to be solemn, and to lift their hearts to God continually in prayer, that we might be prospered. . . .

On getting about half way to Buffalo, the canal broke. This gave rise to much murmuring and discontentment, which was expressed in terms like the following:

"Well, the canal is broke now, and here we are, and here we are likely to be, for we can go no farther. We have left our homes, and here we have no means of getting a living, consequently we shall have to starve."

"No, no," said I, "you will not starve. . . . It is quite probable that the boats cannot leave Buffalo harbor on account of the ice." . . .

. . . As the canal was repaired by eleven o'clock, we proceeded on our journey, and arrived at Buffalo on the fifth day after leaving Waterloo.

Here we found the brethren from Colesville, who informed us that they had been detained one week at this place, waiting for the navigation to open. . . .

I asked them if they had confessed to the people that they were "Mormons." "No, indeed," they replied, "neither must you mention a word about your religion, for if you do you will never be able to get a house, or a boat either."

I told them I should tell the people precisely who I was; "and," continued I, "if you are ashamed of Christ, you must not expect to be prospered; and I shall wonder if we do not get to Kirtland before you." . . .

. . . Captain Blake . . . sent out a man to measure the depth of the ice, who, when he returned, reported that it was piled up to the height of twenty feet, and that it was his opinion that we would remain in the harbor at least two weeks longer. . . .

I went to that part of the boat where the principal portion of our company was. There I found several of the brethren and sisters engaged in a warm debate, others murmuring and grumbling, and a number of young ladies were flirting, giggling, and laughing with gentlemen passengers who were entire strangers to them. . . . I stepped into their midst. ". . . You profess to put your trust in God, then how can you feel to murmur and complain as you do! You are even more unreasonable than the children of Israel were. . . . Where is your faith? Where is your confidence in God?" . . .

. . . "Now, brethren and sisters, if you will all of you raise your desires to heaven, that the ice may be broken up, and we be set at liberty, as sure as the Lord lives, it will be done." At that instant a noise was heard, like bursting thunder. The captain cried, "Every man to his post." The ice parted, leaving barely a passage for the boat, and so narrow that as the boat passed through the buckets of the waterwheel were torn off with a crash, which, joined to the word of command from the captain, the hoarse answering of the sailors, the noise of the ice, and the cries and confusion of the spectators, presented a scene truly terrible. We had barely passed through the avenue when the ice closed together again, and the Colesville brethren were left in Buffalo, unable to follow us. (*History of Joseph Smith by His Mother*, ed. Preston Nibley [Salt Lake City: Bookcraft, 1954], pp. 195–99, 202–5.)

Manna from Heaven

Exodus 16:11–16

And the Lord spake unto Moses, saying,

I have heard the murmurings of the children of Israel: speak unto them, saying, At even ye shall eat flesh, and in the morning ye shall be filled with bread; and ye shall know that I am the Lord your God.

And it came to pass, that at even the quails came up, and covered the camp: and in the morning the dew lay round about the host.

And when the dew that lay was gone up, behold, upon the face of the wilderness there lay a small round thing, as small as the hoar frost on the ground.

And when the children of Israel saw it, they said one to another, It is manna. . . . And Moses said unto them, This is the bread which the Lord hath given you to eat.

This is the thing which the Lord hath commanded, Gather of it every man according to his eating. (Exodus 16:11–16.)

Manna Sugar

Elias H. Blackburn, the first bishop of Provo, related the following experience that occurred in the summer of 1855:

In August, 1855, a memorable blessing was given to the people of Provo in the shape of a hard white substance found upon the leaves of the young cottonwood trees. We shook off this substance, which was very sweet, into tubs of water, and boiled it down, without process, when it congealed into sugar about the color of our common brown sugar. I told the Saints it was a direct gift from the Lord, and they freely paid their tithing on it. Among other products I took 333 lbs. of this sugar to Salt Lake City to the General Tithing Office. On explaining the matter to President Brigham Young, whom I met at the door, he declared it was sugar from the Lord.

Referring to this sugar and other items, the "Deseret News," August 22, 1855, has the following: "Bishop Elias H. Blackburn forwarded to the tithing office in this city, on the 15th inst., by Messrs. Whipple and Riggs, 40 bushels of new potatoes besides other vegetables which were distributed among the Public Hands, and were quite a treat to those whose gardens had been pinched with drouth; also 210 pounds of Manna Sugar, being the tithing on 2100 pounds made from the saccharine deposit upon the leaves of trees. The sugar is a very good quality, much resembling that made from the maple." (In William E. Berrett and Alma P. Burton, *Readings in LDS Church History*, 3 vols. [Salt Lake City: Deseret Book Co., 1953–58], 2:481.)

Gathering of Manna
Forbidden on the Sabbath

Exodus 16:16–24

This is the thing which the Lord hath commanded, Gather of it every man according to his eating, an omer for every man, according to the number of your persons; take ye every man for them which are in his tents. . . .

And Moses said, Let no man leave of it till the morning.

Notwithstanding they hearkened not unto Moses; but some of them left of it until the morning, and it bred worms, and stank: and Moses was wroth with them. . . .

And it came to pass, that on the sixth day they gathered twice as much bread, two omers for one man. . . .

And [Moses] said unto them, This is that which the Lord hath said, To morrow is the rest of the holy sabbath unto the Lord: bake that which ye will bake to day, and seethe that ye will seethe; and that which remaineth over lay up for you to be kept until the morning.

And they laid it up till the morning, as Moses bade: and it did not stink, neither was there any worm therein. (Exodus 16:16, 19–20, 22–24.)

The Hides at the Tannery Never Spoil on Sunday

In talking about the Lord's blessings to those who honor the Sabbath day, Elder James E. Faust taught:

A more recent miracle occurred at the Wells Stake Welfare Tannery some years ago where hides of animals were tanned into leather. On regular work days, the hides were removed from the vats and fresh lime placed in the vats, after which the hides were returned to the lime solution. If the hides were not turned on holidays, they would spoil. But the change was never made on Sunday, and there were no spoiled hides on Monday. Explained J. Lowell Fox, the supervisor of the tannery at the time:

"This brought a strange fact to our minds: holidays are determined by man, and on these days just as on every week day, the hides need to have special care every twelve hours. Sunday is the day set aside by the Lord as a day of rest, and He makes it possible for us to rest from our labors as He has commanded. The hides at the tannery never spoil on Sundays. This is a modern-day miracle, a miracle that happens every weekend!" ("The Lord's Day," *Ensign*, November 1991, p. 35.)

Water Miraculously
Provided from the Rock

Exodus 17:1, 3, 5–6

"And all the congregation of the children of Israel journeyed from the wilderness of Sin, after their journeys, according to the commandment of the Lord, and pitched in Rephidim: and there was no water for the people to drink. . . . And the people thirsted there for water; and the people murmured. . . . And the Lord said unto Moses, Go on before the people, and take with thee of the elders of Israel; and thy rod, wherewith thou smotest the river, take in thine hand, and go. Behold, I will stand before thee there upon the rock in Horeb; and thou shalt smite the rock, and there shall come water out of it, that the people may drink." (Exodus 17:1, 3, 5–6.)

Water Miraculously Provided from the Well

William F. Cahoon, the oldest child of Reynolds Cahoon, was one of those who in 1834 marched with the Prophet Joseph in Zion's Camp from Kirtland, Ohio, to Jackson County, Missouri. William's autobiography and historical records relate the following concerning Zion's Camp:

On May 5, 1834 the Camp left [for] Missouri. It was truly a solemn morning, we left our wives, children and friends, not knowing whether we would see them again as we were threatened by enemies that would destroy and extermi-nate us from the land. We were facing the "lion in his den."

Joseph Smith had made this pledge to us, "If you will go with me to Missouri and keep my counsel, I pledge that I will lead you there and back and not a hair of your head shall be hurt." "This camp," said William F.," marched through a pop-ulation of tens of thousands of people like lambs among wolves, but no man among them opened his mouth to say, 'Why do you do so?' On we marched singing our favorite song, 'Hark listen to the Trumpeters.'" (In *Reynolds Cahoon and His Stalwart Sons*, comp. and ed. Stella Cahoon Shurtleff and Brent Farrington Cahoon [Salt Lake City: Paragon Press, 1960], p. 81.)

Apparently both William F. Cahoon and Zera Cole, who also marched with Zion's Camp, later told Oliver B. Huntington about an incident that occurred during the trek of Zion's Camp. Oliver's account of the incident, based on what he learned from Zera Cole, follows:

The company had traveled in wagons upon the bleak prairies many days, where seldom a house was seen, and they knew very little or nothing of the road; and but occasionally a person was seen who could give correct information of the roads and "by roads." They sometimes camped for a night in a place where comforts were few—such as wood, water and provisions for men; as for feed for their teams, there was plen-ty every where.

One hot day in June, after an unusually long, hard day's travel, over a rolling prairie, without sufficient water laid in for the men and no water encountered for the teams, they made camp on a prairie, the end of which it was impossible to reach or even see.

After tents were pitched and the teams turned out a strong guard had to be placed to keep the animals.

Men were very quietly complaining of the location, the lack of wood, and no water to cook with, even if they had plenty of wood. Some teams were about "give-out" and a thousand other little troubles acted out if not spoken of.

The Prophet sat in his tent door watching and listening to all that could be seen or heard. At last he quietly asked for a spade.

There was no noise, no bustle, no show of greatness or power about this man who had seen the Creator of heaven and earth and had received from Him at different times unmeasured power only in keeping with circumstances, and as the spade was handed him he measured the extent of the camp with his eye and in the most convenient place for all he commenced to dig in the earth. There was no rock to split open, as with Moses of old, or he could have done that more easily and quickly. But he quietly dug a well only a few feet deep and then left it.

Presently the water began to come in, and it kept rising in the well until the mules and horses came and drank there-from, as the water was so near the surface.

The Prophet went and sat in the door of his tent and witnessed the joy of all, even of the animals, as they quenched their thirst in this God-given supply. ("An Incident of Zion's Camp," *Juvenile Instructor*, 1 January 1902, pp. 20–21.)

Who Is on the Lord's Side?

Exodus 32:26

"Then Moses stood in the gate of the camp, and said, Who is on the Lord's side? let him come unto me. And all the sons of Levi gathered themselves together unto him." (Exodus 32:26.)

Hannah Last Cornaby

Hannah Last Cornaby authored the words to the hymn, "Who's on the Lord's Side?" J. Spencer Cornwall related the story of this remarkable woman:

> She was born on 17 March 1822 . . . [in] England. Her parents were devout members of the Episcopal Church, and the Bible was her mother's constant companion. Hannah committed to memory much of the New Testament and the Psalms before she was old enough to read. Good books played an important part in her entire life.
>
> Hannah Last was married to Samuel Cornaby 30 January 1851. . . .
>
> This couple were very dissatisfied with their religion and prayed for guidance in finding a true religion. They owned a bookstore in England. One night during a storm, they saw a man sheltered under the awning of their store. They invited

him in and it so happened he was a Mormon missionary. They were converted to the Church, and Samuel Cornaby was soon baptized. Shortly after the birth of their first child, Hannah requested baptism; and although she received baptism amid a mob of angry people trying to prevent her baptism she says, "We then made our way back, as best we could, followed by the mob; and though the stones whizzed around us thick as hail not one touched us and we reached home safely, thanking God for our miraculous deliverance; determined, more than ever, with the assistance of the holy spirit, to adhere—through evil, as well as good report to the principles we had embraced. At the next meeting of the saints I was confirmed, and knew for myself that the work was of God."

They were so persecuted by their friends that they decided to come to America. . . .

She and her husband walked the entire journey across the plains, and she did not complain. . . .

They arrived in Emigration Canyon 12 Oct. 1853.

They . . . moved to Spanish Fork, Utah, 27 July 1856, where they resided the balance of their lives. (*Stories of Our Mormon Hymns* [Salt Lake City: Deseret Book Co., 1975], pp. 194–95.)

Elsewhere in his sketch of Hannah's life, Cornwall wrote:

Although her life was full of reverses, she always praised God and was never bitter in any way because of any hardship she was called upon to bear. She was an invalid for ten years during which time she was administered to many times through her extended illness. One day Bishop Thurber of Spanish Fork, Utah, came accompanied by Apostle Orson Pratt. The doctors had told her she would never walk again, but Orson Pratt administered to her and promised her she should yet arise from her bed and stand on her feet and be able to go to church again. He also confirmed upon her the gift to write. . . . Although her recovery did not come until fifteen months later, it came suddenly and in a miraculous manner in which she gave all thanks and recognition to God. Following

her recovery she spent the remainder of her life in faithful service and the development and use of her talent to write. . . .

Hannah Cornaby died 1 Sept. 1905 at the age of 83. She
was on the Lord's side from the time she embraced the gospel.
(*Stories of Our Mormon Hymns*, pp. 193–94, 196.)

Face to Face

Exodus 33:11

"And the Lord spake unto Moses face to face, as a man speaketh unto his friend" (Exodus 33:11).

The Face of the Lord

In January 1833 the School of the Prophets was officially organized in Kirtland and began meeting in a room on the upper story of the Newel K. Whitney store, where Joseph Smith was living at the time. Minutes taken by Frederick G. Williams at a March 1833 meeting of the school form the basis of the following excerpt from Joseph Smith's history: "I exhorted the brethren to faithfulness and diligence in keeping the commandments of God, and gave much instruction for the benefit of the Saints, with a promise that the pure in heart should see a heavenly vision; and after remaining a short time in secret prayer, the promise was verified; for many present had the eyes of their understanding opened by the Spirit of God, so as to behold many things. . . . Many of the brethren saw a heavenly vision of the Savior, and concourses of angels, and many other things, of which each one has a record of what he saw." (*History of the Church* 1:334–35.)

One of those who attended the School of the Prophets, Zebedee Coltrin, later described what he saw while members of the school were praying: "I saw a personage passing through the room as plainly as I see you now [the high priests at Spanish Fork]. Joseph asked us if we knew who it was and answered himself, 'That is Jesus, our elder brother, the Son of God.'" After the vision closed, the Prophet instructed the men to resume praying, which they did. Zebedee recalled what happened: "Again I saw passing through the same room, a personage whose glory and brightness was so great, that I can liken it to nothing but the burning bush that Moses saw, and its power was so great that had it continued much longer I believe it would have consumed us." After this personage had disappeared, Joseph Smith declared that they had seen "the Father of Jesus Christ." Zebedee Coltrin concluded his testimony by saying, "I saw him." (High Priests Records of Spanish Fork, 5 February 1878, Archives Division, Church Historical Department, The Church of Jesus Christ of Latter-day Saints, Salt Lake City, Utah [hereafter cited as LDS Church Archives]; Minutes of Salt Lake School of the Prophets, 3 October 1883, p. 60, LDS Church Archives.)

Another man, John Murdock, left this testimony:

> During the winter that I boarded with Brother Joseph [1833] . . . , we had a number of prayer meetings, in the Prophet's chamber, in which we obtained great blessings. In one of these meetings the Prophet told us if we could humble ourselves before God, and exercise strong faith, we should see the face of the Lord. And about midday the visions of my mind were opened, and the eyes of my understanding were enlightened, and I saw the form of a man, most lovely, the visage of his face was sound and fair as the sun. His hair a bright silver gray, curled in most majestic form. His eyes a keen penetrating blue, and the skin of his neck a most beautiful white and he was covered from the neck to the feet with a loose garment, pure white, whiter than any garment I have ever before seen. His countenance was most penetrating, and yet most lovely. And while I was endeavoring to comprehend the whole personage from head to feet it slipped from me,

and the vision was closed up. But it left on my mind the
impression of love, for months, that I never felt before that
degree. (Journal of John Murdock, 1833, LDS Church
Archives; see also Elder Loren C. Dunn, "Did Not Our Heart
Burn Within Us?" *Ensign*, May 1977, p. 30.)

Rain in Due Season

Leviticus 26:3–4

"If ye walk in my statutes, and keep my commandments, and do them; then I will give you rain in due season, and the land shall yield her increase, and the trees of the field shall yield their fruit" (Leviticus 26:3–4).

Prayers and Fasting Bring Rain

Chile is a long, narrow land along the west coast of South America. It has large desert areas and is generally quite dry. For water, the Chilean families depend mainly upon the snow which falls in the high Andes mountains. Reservoirs and water pipelines are very important. Rainfall is also important to help water the crops and to supply drinking water for the people and animals.

Some years are very dry, with little rain and snowfall. Beginning in the early months of 1968, Chile experienced a terrible drought. Month after month, there was no rainfall. The snow had almost completely disappeared, even in the high mountains. Crops dried up, cattle died, and one by one reservoirs dried up. In some areas, drinking water had to be hauled for long distances.

People of many faiths prayed earnestly. The Latter-day Saints fasted and prayed and patiently waited upon the Lord.

They knew of the story from pioneer times when the faith of the Saints brought the seagulls to destroy the crickets and save the crops. The Chilean Saints had faith that the Lord would bless their beloved land.

The dry months continued. It had been more than twelve months since it had rained.

Scientists from many nations came to Chile to study the situation. These were men skilled in forecasting the weather many months into the future. Finally, they prepared a statement of their findings. The people were shocked and saddened when they read the headlines: "Drought will continue for another year."

For many, this news was unbearable, but the Saints continued to fast and pray.

Then a wonderful event was announced. Elder Gordon B. Hinckley, a member of the Council of the Twelve Apostles, would soon visit Chile to dedicate two chapels.

Elder Hinckley had visited Chile before, and he loved the people and their beautiful country. He had remembered flying over the snowcapped mountains. This time he was shocked by the dryness of the mountains. Elder Hinckley shook his head in sorrow and sympathy at the sight of dry, brown hills and fields. "Where is the snow in the Andes?" he asked. When he was told about the suffering of the people, tears filled his eyes.

As Elder Hinckley dedicated one of the chapels, he prayed with great faith that the Lord would bring moisture to Chile. All who were in attendance were deeply moved by the powerful prayer of a living Apostle of the Lord. Some said that if Elder Hinckley had not had great faith, he would not have dared to pray for rain. After all, the wisest experts had already predicted another rainless year. But the Saints had faith that Elder Hinckley had been inspired to ask the Lord for this blessing.

The following day, Elder Hinckley flew to Argentina for a meeting. When he returned to Chile, he spoke again of the dry mountains. He could hardly believe they were so dry.

A day or two later, Elder Hinckley traveled several hundred miles south, where he dedicated the new chapel in Talcahuano. Again, in his dedicatory prayer, he pled fervently for rain.

The very next day the gentle rains began to fall in Talcahuano and in many parts of southern Chile. Within a few days, the rain spread into the populous area around Santiago. Snow once more began to cover the Andes. Antofagasta in the far north, where almost no rain had fallen for over forty years, received two heavy downpours.

Elder Hinckley's prayer and the prayers and fasting of the Saints had been answered with a bounteous blessing. The scientists were amazed, but the Saints had no doubt that the Lord was the source of their blessings. (Told by Robert H. Burton, former mission president in Chile, in *Walk in His Ways: Basic Manual for Children, Part B* [Salt Lake City: The Church of Jesus Christ of Latter-day Saints, 1979], pp. 140–42.)

Quails from the
Lord for Israel

Numbers 11:31–32

"And there went forth a wind from the Lord, and brought quails from the sea, and let them fall by the camp, as it were a day's journey on this side, and as it were a day's journey on the other side, round about the camp, and as it were two cubits high upon the face of the earth. And the people stood up all that day, and all that night, and all the next day, and they gathered the quails: he that gathered least gathered ten homers: and they spread them all abroad for themselves round about the camp." (Numbers 11:31–32.)

Quails from the Lord for the Saints

As the pioneers were driven from Nauvoo in 1846, many were not very prepared for the journey across Iowa. Heavy rains fell and turned the roads into mud holes. Temperatures dropped, and with their clothes and bedding drenched, the Saints experienced frequent illnesses and occasional deaths that hindered travel.

By mid-March over two thousand Saints had left Nauvoo and were trekking across Iowa. Hundreds more left in April and May. But many were still in Nauvoo and unable to get away.

All through the summer, enemies persecuted the remaining

Saints. They rode through grain fields, at times attacking and severely beating Church members. This harassment continued into the fall of 1846. Then, in September, the anti-Mormons attacked Nauvoo, determined to drive the Saints away. Those who could fled quickly across the Mississippi River for safety. Unfortunately, however, they were without provisions or additional clothing.

Refugee camps of five to six hundred displaced men, women, and children were scattered along the riverbank near Montrose, Iowa. The fortunate ones had blankets. Most slept in huts made of brush for shelter.

On October 9, when food was in critically short supply, several large flocks of quail flew into the camp and landed on the ground and even on the tables of the Saints. Many of them were caught, cooked, and eaten. The beleaguered Saints recognized it as a miracle and a sign of God's mercy on modern Israel.

Writing about their experience, Elder Thomas Bullock described this most fortunate miracle:

> On the 9th of October several wagons with oxen having been sent by the Twelve to fetch the poor Saints away, were drawn out in a line on the river banks ready to start. But hark! what is that? See! the quails descend. They alight close by our little camp of twelve wagons, run past each wagon tongue, when they arise, fly around the camp three times, descend and again run the gauntlet past each wagon. See! the sick knock them down with sticks and the little children catch them alive with their hands! Some are cooked for breakfast.
>
> While my family were seated on the wagon tongue and ground, having a washtub for a table, behold they come again! One descends upon our tea-board in the midst of our cups, while we were actually around the table eating our breakfast, which a little boy eight years old catched alive with his hands. They rise again, the flocks increase in number, seldom going seven rods from our camp, continually flying around the camp, sometimes under the wagons, sometimes over, and even into the wagons where the poor, sick

Saints are lying in bed; thus having a direct manifestation from the Most High that although we are driven by men He has not forsaken us, but that His eyes are continually over us for good. At noon, having caught alive about fifty and killed about fifty more, the captain gave orders not to kill any more, as it was a direct manifestation and visitation from the Lord. In the afternoon hundreds were flying at a time. When our camp started at three p.m. there could not have been less than five hundred, some said there were fifteen hundred, flying around the camp.

Thus am I a witness to this visitation. Some Gentiles who were at the camp marveled greatly. Even passengers on a steamboat going down the river looked with astonishment. (In William E. Berrett and Alma P. Burton, *Readings in LDS Church History*, 3 vols. [Salt Lake City: Deseret Book Co., 1953–58], 2:193–94.)

Thy People Shall Be My People

Ruth 1:1–17

Naomi, her husband, Elimelech, and their two sons left their home in Bethlehem due to a terrible famine. They settled in the land of Moab. Elimelech later died, and Naomi's two sons married. Then both of her sons died, and Naomi was left with her daughters-in-law to care for themselves. She announced her intention to return to her home in Bethlehem, and she "said unto her two daughters in law, Go, return each to her mother's house: the Lord deal kindly with you, as ye have dealt with the dead, and with me. The Lord grant you that ye may find rest, each of you in the house of her husband. Then she kissed them; and they lifted up their voice, and wept."

One of the women left and returned to her own family. But Ruth remained, saying, "Intreat me not to leave thee, or to return from following after thee: for whither thou goest, I will go; and where thou lodgest, I will lodge: thy people shall be my people, and thy God my God." (See Ruth 1:1–17.)

Because she went with Naomi, Ruth had the privilege of remarrying in the covenant and was blessed to preserve the family line through which the Messiah would be born.

Willingness to Sacrifice All for the Gospel Brings Greater Blessings

Daniel Hanmer Wells, a prominent citizen in Illinois,

befriended the Saints who were driven from Missouri. He was married to Eliza Robinson, and they were the parents of one child, Albert. Though not a member of the Church at that time, he sold the property to Joseph Smith on which the Nauvoo Temple would be constructed and did all he could to help the Saints settle in their new home.

Daniel was close to the Saints, but his wife and his son would have nothing to do with the Church. As Annie Wells Cannon, a daughter of Daniel's by a later marriage, explained, the fact that Daniel refrained from being baptized for many years "was not due to a lack of knowledge and faith in Mormonism, but to a belief that he could render the people better service as a non-Mormon public official, as well as to the opposition of his family, which he hoped to overcome" (in Bryant S. Hinckley, *Daniel Hanmer Wells and Events of His Time* [Salt Lake City: Deseret News Press, 1942], p. 343).

After Joseph and Hyrum were murdered, the Saints were again persecuted and eventually driven from Nauvoo during the first part of 1846. For various reasons, however, many Saints still remained in the city. In August of that year, Daniel, also still in Nauvoo, was baptized. Determined to clear the remaining Saints out of Nauvoo, enemies of the Church formed to lay siege to the city in September. The result was the Battle of Nauvoo, in which Daniel Wells, now a member of the Church, fought valiantly. Nevertheless, the siege forced the evacuation of almost all the remaining Saints from Nauvoo. Among those who left were Daniel Wells and his family, who stayed for a time in Burlington, Iowa, and then moved to Galesburg, Illinois, till the early part of 1848.

Daniel longed to be with the Saints. Ruth's words to Naomi described his anguish, "Intreat me not to leave thee." And he was constrained to decide between his love for the Lord and his love for his family, who refused to move. No persuasion on Daniel's part could prevail upon his wife's feelings. Wrote Rulon S. Wells, Daniel's fourth son, "He was therefore compelled to leave her behind or renounce Mormonism, to which he was now convert-ed." As he left to join the main body of the Saints, he gave his wife and his son all of his property, which was considerable, to ensure they would be well provided for, and took with him, wrote Rulon, "only enough to barely outfit himself for the trip across the plains." (In Hinckley, *Daniel Hanmer Wells*, p. 365.)

In a letter to President Brigham Young in 1848, just prior to his departure from Illinois, Daniel H. Wells wrote about his distress: "I see no prospect short of a complete sacrifice of everything I hold dear on earth, as well in a pecuniary point of view, as the kindlier affections of the human heart. Please to remember me before the Lord that I may be sustained through the dark day and at least one ray of light may beam into my soul, to cheer me on the way. Think not that I am desponding or despairing, for though my soul is bowed down under a great weight of afflictions, yet my faith is placed upon the Lord of hosts, and 'come weal, come wo,' I will be with you by the 1st of April, or sooner if possible."

Following is Brigham Young's response:

Dear Brother Wells:

I feel to sympathize with you in your afflictions, yet you are aware by this time that those who will serve the Lord will sacrifice everything, whether it be land or possessions, or pecuniary interest or the kindlier affections of the heart, and inasmuch as you do this to the glory of God, you will in no wise lose your reward in this world, and in the world to come you will receive eternal life, glory and immortality. Cheer up your heart, and rejoice in the day of your deliverance, and comfort your heart that my prayer is offered up in your behalf, and may the time soon arrive that we shall be able to strike hands and go on our way rejoicing to a land of peace, happiness and holiness, that we may all enjoy health and strength and do the will of him that sent us.

Accept the assurance of
Your faithful brother in Christ,

Brigham Young

Writer Bryant S. Hinckley described the impact of this letter on Daniel H. Wells: "This inspiring letter from Brigham Young was a source of great consolation to Daniel H. Wells in those dark days. He left Nauvoo in 1848, never to return, nor did he ever again see his wife or his son. In the tragedy and suffering which accompanied the banishments of the Saints from Illinois, no other man bore a heavier part." (*Daniel Hanmer Wells*, pp. 48–49.)

Daniel eventually remarried and had a large posterity. He was later called to serve as a Counselor to President Brigham Young in the First Presidency. One of his sons, Heber M. Wells, became the first governor in the state of Utah, and one of his daughters, Emily, married President Heber J. Grant. As Rulon Wells pointed out, though Daniel's first son, Albert, "attained the ripe old age of seventy-six years he never married and therefore had it not been for the sacrifice made in [1848] the final death of his son would have been the end of [Daniel's] posterity" (in Hinckley, *Daniel Hanmer Wells*, p. 366).

Referring to his father's leaving behind family and property to join the Saints, Rulon also wrote: "In this episode of father's life, the following scripture is literally fulfilled: 'And Jesus answered and said, Verily I say unto you, There is no man that hath left house, or brethren, or sisters, or father, or mother, or wife, or children, or lands, for my sake, and the Gospel's but he shall receive an hundredfold now in this time, houses, and brethren, and sisters, and mothers, and children, and lands, with persecutions; and in the world to come eternal life' (Mark 10:29–30)." (In Hinckley, *Daniel Hanmer Wells*, p. 365.)

Listening to the Voice of the Lord

1 Samuel 3:8–10

"And the Lord called Samuel again the third time. And he arose and went to Eli, and said, Here am I; for thou didst call me. And Eli perceived that the Lord had called the child. Therefore Eli said unto Samuel, Go, lie down: and it shall be, if he call thee, that thou shalt say, Speak, Lord; for thy servant heareth. So Samuel went and lay down in his place. And the Lord came, and stood, and called as at other times, Samuel, Samuel. Then Samuel answered, Speak; for thy servant heareth." (1 Samuel 3:8–10.)

We often live beneath our privileges. Hesitancy to follow the promptings of the Spirit can cost us some wonderful opportunities and cause us to forfeit great blessings.

Lorenzo Dow Young

In March, 1833, I removed to Kirtland. The Kirtland Temple committee was appointed June 6th, 1833. About that time, I took with my team Brothers Hyrum and Joseph Smith, Reynolds Cahoon and my brother Brigham, to look at a stone quarry, and see if the rock was suitable for walls of the temple. It was decided that it would do, and a part of a load was put on the wagon. . . .

From that time I worked with the brethren, as occasion required, until the temple was completed. On the 17th of February, 1834, those holding the Priesthood were called together to organize a High Council. I was one of the number. On that occasion I committed a great error. That it may be a lesson for others, is my reason for relating it here. The Prophet requested me to take a seat with other brethren who had been selected for this Council.

Instead of doing as requested, I arose and plead my inability to fill so responsible a position, manifesting, I think, considerable earnestness in the matter. The Prophet then said that he really desired that I should take the place.

Still excusing myself, he appointed another to fill it. I think this was the reason the Prophet never again called me to fill any important position in the Priesthood during his life.

I have since learned to go where I am called, and not set up my judgment against that of those who are called to lead in this kingdom. (Lorenzo Dow Young, "Lorenzo Dow Young's Narrative," in *Fragments of Experience* [Salt Lake City: Juvenile Instructor Office, 1882], pp. 42–43. *Fragments of Experience* was reprinted as part of the 4-vols.-in-1 publication *Four Faith-Promoting Classics* [Salt Lake City: Bookcraft, 1968].)

To his eternal credit, Lorenzo Dow Young stayed true to the Church and to the Prophet Joseph Smith. He arrived in Salt Lake City with the original 1847 company of pioneers (in fact, his wife, Harriet Wheeler, was one of only three women allowed to travel with that first company). Within a short time he was called by President Brigham Young to serve as one of the first bishops in the Salt Lake Valley, a position he faithfully held for many years.

Patriarchal Promises Require Obedience

I recall a story which President Lee told about a man who had been called by a member of the First Presidency to serve as a mission president. This man was an extremely successful business man with major business affairs. He told the member of the First Presidency that he would like to think over the calling before giving his answer. The man called a member of the Council of the Twelve and inquired as to what he thought he should do about the call to be a mission president. The apostle told him that he thought he didn't have any choice; he should willingly serve in any capacity the Lord desired. The man called a second apostle and received a similar response. Then he called a third and a fourth apostle; all of their answers were the same.

Finally the brother told the member of the First Presidency that he would accept the calling. The member of the First Presidency replied that they had already called someone else. "Perhaps you will be called again in the future," he said.

The man then went to President Harold B. Lee, then a member of the Quorum of the Twelve, and told him that the mission presidency call had been revoked. "My patriarchal blessing tells me that I will be a General Authority someday," the businessman said. "Do you think my delaying the answer to the call so long that it was revoked will have any effect upon my patriarchal blessing promise?" President Lee simply answered that he did not know.

Several months later President Lee sat in a Quorum of the Twelve meeting where names of men to serve as General Authorities were being suggested. President Lee later said that he turned pale as he heard this man's name considered and then passed over. (Vaughn J. Featherstone, *Do-It-Yourself Destiny* [Salt Lake City: Bookcraft, 1977], pp. 168–69.)

Israel's Enemies Are Subdued by the Lord

1 Samuel 7:10

"And as Samuel was offering up the burnt offering, the Philistines drew near to battle against Israel: but the Lord thundered with a great thunder on that day upon the Philistines, and discomfited them; and they were smitten before Israel" (1 Samuel 7:10).

Zion's Camp Miraculously Protected at Fishing River

After marching almost a thousand miles in the most trying conditions, Joseph and the brethren of Zion's Camp arrived near Jackson County in June 1834. One of the most dramatic events of Zion's Camp occurred while the company was stopped on a hill between the two main branches of Fishing River between Richmond and Liberty, Missouri. Five men representing the mob rode into the camp and swore terrible oaths against the brethren, threatening that they would kill them. "Such horrible oaths as came from their lips I never heard before," recalled Heber C. Kimball, a member of the camp. The five boasted that sixty men were coming from Richmond and another seventy from Clay County to join the already organized mob of about two hundred camped just across the river. Heber wrote, "The whole county was in a rage against us, and nothing but the power of God could save us." (Quoted in Orson F. Whitney, *Life of Heber C. Kimball* [1888; reprint, Salt Lake City: Bookcraft, 1992], p. 52.)

The members of Zion's Camp were hemmed in on two sides by the steep banks of Fishing River. The Prophet Joseph's history describes the miracle that occurred as the Lord "discomfited" Israel's enemies that night:

> When these five men were in our camp, swearing vengeance, the wind, thunder, and rising cloud indicated an approaching storm, and in a short time after they left the rain and hail began to fall. The storm was tremendous; wind and rain, hail and thunder met them in great wrath, and soon softened their direful courage, and frustrated all their designs to "kill Joe Smith and his army." Instead of continuing a cannonading which they commenced when the sun was about one hour high, they crawled under wagons, into hollow trees, and filled one old shanty, till the storm was over, when their ammunition was soaked, and the forty in Clay county were extremely anxious in the morning to return to Jackson, having experienced the pitiless pelting of the storm all night; and as soon as arrangements could be made, this "forlorn hope" took the "back track" for Independence, to join the main body of the mob, fully satisfied, as were those survivors of the company who were drowned, that when Jehovah fights they would rather be absent. The gratification is too terrible.
>
> Very little hail fell in our camp, but from half a mile to a mile around, the stones or lumps of ice cut down the crops of corn and vegetation generally, even cutting limbs from trees, while the trees, themselves were twisted into withes by the wind. The lightning flashed incessantly, which caused it to be so light in our camp through the night, that we could discern the most minute objects; and the roaring of the thunder was tremendous. The earth trembled and quaked, the rain fell in torrents, and, united, it seemed as if the mandate of vengeance had gone forth from the God of battles, to protect His servants from the destruction of their enemies, for the hail fell on them and not on us, and we suffered no harm, except the blowing down of some of our tents, and getting wet; while our enemies had holes made in their hats, and

otherwise received damage, even the breaking of their rifle stocks, and the fleeing of their horses through fear and pain.

Many of my little band sheltered in an old meetinghouse through this night, and in the morning the water in Big Fishing river was about forty feet deep, where, the previous evening, it was no more than to our ankles, and our enemies swore that the water rose thirty feet in thirty minutes in the Little Fishing river. They reported that one of their men was killed by lightning, and that another had his hand torn off by his horse drawing his hand between the logs of a corn crib while he was holding him on the inside. They declared that if that was the way God fought for the Mormons, they might as well go about their business. (*History of the Church* 2:103–5.)

Wilford Woodruff added this testimony: "We all fled into a Baptist meetinghouse. As the Prophet Joseph came in shaking the water from his hat and clothing he said, 'Boys, there is some meaning to this. God is in this storm.' We sang praises to God, and lay all night on benches under cover while our enemies were in the pelting storm. . . . It was reported that the captain of the company . . . said it was a strange thing that they could do nothing against the Mormons but what there must be some hail storm or some other thing to hinder their doing anything, but they did not feel disposed to acknowledge that God was fighting our battles." (*History of the Church* 2:104n.)

The Lord Looks on the Heart

1 Samuel 16:7

"But the Lord said unto Samuel, Look not on his countenance, or on the height of his stature; because I have refused him: for the Lord seeth not as man seeth; for man looketh on the outward appearance, but the Lord looketh on the heart" (1 Samuel 16:7).

No Visible Blemish

I have a friend who served as a priests quorum adviser. The boys and the adviser planned a kayak activity at Flaming Gorge, Utah. After some initial planning, one of the quorum members quietly approached the adviser and said: "We better not plan a kayak trip. Mike won't be able to go because he can't paddle." Mike was partially paralyzed on his right side. When he learned the quorum was not going on the activity because of him, he told the boys, "I want to go. I can paddle." The quorum adviser placed his hand on Mike's shoulder and said, "OK, Mike. You're my paddle partner."

So from January to August, the boys built their kayaks. They departed to the reservoir in the first week in August.

Rhythm, togetherness, and teamwork are essential to keep a kayak in a straight line. Mike and his partner had more trouble than the others getting their rhythm and strokes coordinated. Mike had almost no stroke of consequence on his right side. His adviser had to compensate by paddling easy on the left and hard on the right.

After several hours of learning to work together, Mike said to his adviser, "You wouldn't happen to have a Band-Aid, would you?" The adviser pulled his wallet out and gave Mike a Band-Aid. He placed it over a big water blister that had just popped in the crook of his hand between his thumb and his first finger. The hand and arm that was little used now had to help hold the paddle.

Several hours later, Mike turned again to his adviser, who was in the rear cockpit, and said, "Do you have any more bandages?" The adviser pulled out several and handed them to Mike. By now the crook between Mike's right thumb and his first finger was becoming raw. Mike applied the Band-Aids and resumed paddling.

The next day the crew set out again. The adviser encouraged Mike to rest from paddling and let his hand have a respite. The words fell on deaf ears. Instantly, Mike was paddling as he had the day before.

This day found a usual midday and afternoon wind blowing directly at the flotilla of kayak paddlers. It required stronger strokes and took much energy and time. Wincing from the hurt, Mike continued to paddle. Each suggestion that he rest intensified his will to carry his load.

Throughout the week, Mike persisted in holding his own. Though his hand was as raw as hamburger and awful to look at, he would not give up.

During the week's trip, the conversation with his senior companion often centered around his desire to go on a mission. Repeatedly Mike asked, "I hope they will let me go on a mission. Do you think my problem will prevent me from going?" Mike walks with a noticeable limp of his right leg. He has a firm handshake with the left hand, but his right hand doesn't open up all of the way.

How many who have no visible blemish have a heart like Mike's? How many young men with not a single cell out of place fail to soften their hearts and desire to serve the

Lord? How many who have so much forfeit their blessings because of selfish desires or inability to set lofty priorities?

My adviser friend said, "Mike taught eleven others that though one may appear to be a little less physically capable, the heart makes the difference in those who choose to overcome many odds and set a standard for others to follow."

Mike fulfilled an honorable mission to California and is now working in his hometown. (Marvin J. Ashton, "The Measure of Our Hearts," *Ensign*, November 1988, p. 16.)

David Escapes Messengers Sent to Kill Him

1 Samuel 19:18–24

After David escaped from Saul through the help of David's wife, Michal, David sought refuge with Samuel in Ramah. Saul sent messengers to take David, but when the messengers and finally Saul himself came to Ramah, they came under the influence of the Spirit, and David's life was spared.

"And Saul sent messengers to take David: and when they saw the company of the prophets prophesying, and Samuel standing as appointed over them, the Spirit of God was upon the messengers of Saul, and they also prophesied. And when it was told Saul, he sent other messengers, and they prophesied likewise. And Saul sent messengers again the third time, and they prophesied also. Then went he also to Ramah, . . . and he asked and said, Where are Samuel and David? And one said, Behold, they be at Naioth in Ramah. And he went thither . . . : and the Spirit of God was upon him also, and he went on, and prophesied." (See 1 Samuel 19:18–24.)

Wilford Woodruff Delivered While Serving a Mission in England

When I arose to speak at Brother Benbow's house, a man entered the door and informed me that he was a constable, and had been sent by the rector of the parish with a warrant to arrest me. I asked him, "For what crime?" He said, "For preaching to the people." I told him that I, as well as the rector, had a license for preaching the gospel to the people, and that if he would take a chair I would wait upon him after meeting. He took my chair and sat beside me. For an hour and a quarter I preached the first principles of the everlasting gospel. The power of God rested upon me, the spirit filled the house, and the people were convinced. At the close of the meeting I opened the door for baptism, and seven offered themselves. Among the number were four preachers and the constable. The latter arose and said, "Mr. Woodruff, I would like to be baptized." I told him I would like to baptize him. I went down into the pool and baptized the seven. We then came together. I confirmed thirteen, administered the Sacrament and we all rejoiced together.

The constable went to the rector and told him that if he wanted Mr. Woodruff taken for preaching the gospel, he must go himself and serve the writ; for he had heard him preach the only true gospel sermon he had ever listened to in his life. The rector did not know what to make of it, so he sent two clerks of the Church of England as spies, to attend our meeting, and find out what we did preach. They both were pricked in their hearts, received the word of the Lord gladly, and were baptized and confirmed members of the Church of Jesus Christ of Latter-day Saints. The rector became alarmed, and did not venture to send anybody else. (Wilford Woodruff, as cited in Matthias F. Cowley, *Wilford Woodruff: History of His Life and Labors* [Salt Lake City: Bookcraft, 1964], p. 118.)

Wisdom Comes
with Age

1 Kings 12:1–17

After King Solomon died, the kingdom of Israel was divided when a disagreement arose between Solomon's sons, Rehoboam and Jeroboam. Rehoboam sought to place greater burdens on the people, in spite of their pleas for mercy: "Thy father made our yoke grievous: now therefore make thou the grievous service of thy father, and his heavy yoke which he put upon us, lighter, and we will serve thee."

King Rehoboam consulted with "the old men, that stood before Solomon his father, . . . and said, How do ye advise that I may answer this people?" With the wisdom that comes only with age, they counseled him, "If thou wilt be a servant unto this people this day, and wilt serve them, and answer them, and speak good words to them, then they will be thy servants for ever."

But Rehoboam "forsook the counsel of the old men, which they had given him, and consulted with the young men that were grown up with him, and which stood before him." They told him to come down even harder on the people than his father had. So "the king answered the people roughly, and forsook the old men's counsel that they gave him." The result was that the northern ten tribes revolted and turned to Rehoboam's brother, Jeroboam, for leadership. (See 1 Kings 12:1–17.)

That was three thousand years ago, and the house of Israel is just now being gathered back together through missionary work.

About Crows

Although not a story, the following poem (whose authorship is unknown) contains teachings that parallel King Rehoboam's experience:

The old crow is getting slow.
The young crow is not.
Of what the young crow does now know,
The old crow knows a lot.

As knowing things, the old crow
Is still the young crow's master.
What does the slow old crow not know?
How to go faster!

The young crow flies above, below,
And rings around the slow old crow.
What does the fast young crow not know?
Where to go!

The Widow's Barrel of Meal

1 Kings 17:8–16

And the word of the Lord came unto [Elijah], saying,

Arise, get thee to Zarephath, which belongeth to Zidon, and dwell there: behold, I have commanded a widow woman there to sustain thee.

. . . And when he came to the gate of the city, behold, the widow woman was there gathering of sticks: and he called to her, and said, Fetch me, I pray thee, a little water in a vessel, that I may drink.

And as she was going to fetch it, he called to her, and said, Bring me, I pray thee, a morsel of bread in thine hand.

And she said, As the Lord thy God liveth, I have not a cake, but an handful of meal in a barrel, and a little oil in a cruse: and, behold, I am gathering two sticks, that I may go in and dress it for me and my son, that we may eat it, and die.

And Elijah said unto her, Fear not; go and do as thou hast said: but make me thereof a little cake first, and bring it unto me, and after make for thee and for thy son.

For thus saith the Lord God of Israel, The barrel of meal shall not waste, neither shall the cruse of oil fail, until the day that the Lord sendeth rain upon the earth.

And she went and did according to the saying of Elijah: and she, and he, and her house, did eat many days.

And the barrel of meal wasted not, neither did the cruse of oil fail, according to the word of the Lord, which he spake by Elijah. (1 Kings 17:8–16.)

A Shovelful of Coal

World War II had been over almost two years, but we were still on rations.

It was February 1947, one of the hardest winters anyone could remember. Our home town of Bradford, Yorkshire, England, was the coldest spot in the nation, and it had snowed off and on for six weeks.

By now the drifted snow was higher than our heads—that meant no cart could reach us to deliver our ration of coal. And we were running low.

There were six of us living together that winter—my husband and I, our two children, a young man who had been turned out of his own home when he joined the Church, and a woman whose daughter was serving a mission. We did our best to keep warm, but we were almost out of fuel and we only had electricity at certain hours during the day. (Most of our power stations had been badly bombed during the war.)

It was Saturday when my husband went down to the cellar and carefully sifted the coal from the dust. All that remained was one shovelful of coal and a few cans of coal dust.

At church the next day, we received a shopping bag full of wood. The elders had sawed the wood from old railroad ties and stored it in the basement of the church. With this wood and our little pile of coal, we had fuel enough for one more day.

That evening we knelt in prayer and asked the Lord to help us. As we prayed, our helplessness gave way to a sense of peace. When we went to bed, we felt content to leave the situation in the Lord's hands.

On Monday morning I put some wood, a can of dust, and the remaining coal into the fireplace. Then I waited until afternoon to start the fire—I wanted the house to be as warm as possible when the children got home from school.

The fire lasted until nine or ten that night. We were amazed to discover that all six of us kept warm and comfortable from the one little fire through the entire evening. My husband added a can of dust and one log, but that was all.

The next morning I cleaned out the fireplace and began

to lay paper and wood as I had the day before. Then I plucked up my courage and faith and went down to the cellar. Not knowing quite what to except, I opened the door. There, in the same corner where it had been yesterday, was a stack of coal that looked just like the coal we had burned the night before. I had the strangest feeling—had an angel brought it? I had no answer for my question, but reverently scooped up the coal and took it upstairs.

How grateful we were that night for our miraculous fire. Our prayers were prayers of appreciation and praise.

The next morning when I went down to the cellar I found another stack of coal in the same corner. It was just enough. This miracle occurred every day that week until Saturday. By that time my husband felt that the snow had melted enough so that he would finally be able to get us some coal. . . .

I still have no explanation for this incident. All I know is that it did happen and six of us witnessed it. And we knew that God lives and answers prayers. (Marjorie A. McCormick, "One Shovelful of Coal," *Ensign*, October 1979, pp. 49–50.)

Two Bags of Cement

In June 1964, we were pouring the concrete floors in the chapel and recreational hall of the Poverty Bay District and Gisborne [New Zealand] Second Branch Chapel. There had been storms in the area for three weeks and the boats had not been able to deliver cement to Gisborne. We had borrowed all the cement there was within eighty miles, and when we quit work for lunch on the last day of pouring, we had just two bags of cement left and needed two and a half yards of concrete—enough to fill an area fifteen feet by thirteen feet. This would have required twelve bags of concrete to complete the job. As we returned from lunch everyone was saying, "We may as well not even start again; it wouldn't even be worthwhile."

I told them to start the mixer; that we were not only going to pour, but we would complete our floors that day. Then, not knowing at the time how it could be done, I walked a short distance from the group and prayed. I simply said, "Father you fed the thousands with the five loaves and two fishes. Surely you can help us this day."

We went to work and mixed two small one-fourth yard batches of concrete with the two bags of cement we had and started pouring. There seemed to be no end to the concrete as it poured from our wheelbarrows. The full pour was not only completed, but we had to remove two wheelbarrows full when it was leveled out.

There is no physical way this could have been done by men. It was indeed a modern miracle performed for his people of the latter days. (John Purser, in Margie Calhoun Jensen, *When Faith Writes the Story* [Salt Lake City: Bookcraft, 1973], p. 69.)

Job and Adversity

Job 19:25–26

In a 1978 fireside address at Brigham Young University, Presiding Bishop Victor L. Brown alluded to the experience of Job:

> The story is told of a very wealthy man who had a lovely family of seven children and who was living a righteous life. Because of adversity, he lost his wealth. His children died. His wife turned against him, and his friends made light of him. His body was racked with illness. His soul was tormented—and yet, because he desired to return to the presence of his Heavenly Father above all else, he kept the faith. After all this, he said:
>
> For I know that my redeemer liveth, and that he shall stand at the latter day upon the earth:
>
> And though after my skin worms destroy this body, yet in my flesh shall I see God. . . .
>
> All the while my breath is in me, and the spirit of God is in my nostrils;
>
> My lips shall not speak wickedness, nor my tongue utter deceit.
>
> God forbid that I should justify you [speaking of his critical friends]: till I die I will not remove mine integrity from me. (Job 19:25–26; 27:3–5.)

It Isn't Always Easy

In the same address quoted above, Bishop Brown related the following experience:

> I was attending a stake conference; and on Saturday afternoon between meetings, when we normally have a bite to eat, the stake president asked if he might be excused to visit his wife in the hospital. This was the first I knew that she was ill. Upon further inquiry I found that she was critically ill. As a matter of fact, the doctors indicated that she had just a few more hours to live. I, of course, told the stake president that he was excused from any further responsibilities for the conference, whereupon he said his wife had told him that his responsibility at that time was to carry out his priesthood obligation and that she preferred that he attend to his stake conference responsibilities.
>
> He went to the hospital and then returned to our seven o'clock meeting. At the conclusion of this meeting, he went back to the hospital and stayed all night by her bedside. He arrived promptly at our meeting Sunday morning and delivered an unusually fine address to the members of the stake. The only time his emotions broke—and then just slightly—was when I suggested that for the intermediate song we sing "I Need Thee Every Hour."
>
> After the conference was over, I went alone to the hospital to meet a woman who so loved the Lord and her husband as to encourage him to honor his priesthood even under the most trying of circumstances. As I came to her room, I was greeted by her returned missionary son who was by her side. She seemed to be sleeping, so I left. As I returned to my car, her son hurried after me and said that she had roused and asked if I would come back to give her a blessing.
>
> As I walked into her room, I saw lying on the bed a lovely, beautiful young mother. I do not think she had any gray hair. She had a lovely smile on her face, even though she was so sick. When I expressed my admiration for her faith and reminded her of the blessings she had stored in heaven, she smiled and said, "Bishop Brown, it isn't always easy, but the Lord truly blesses us."

This good woman had gone through all of the anguish and difficulties of a long siege of cancer, including many operations. Her life was ebbing very rapidly; and yet under these circumstances, realizing full well that it would not be very long before she would face the sorrow of leaving a lovely family, she had the faith and the strength to encourage her husband to do his duty—which really means that she was influencing him in an unusual way to order his life so that he, too, would achieve eternal life.

The next morning early she quietly passed away. As a righteous wife and mother, she had qualified herself to enjoy the blessings of eternal life. She truly loved the Lord and had proven her love after deep trial, as had Job. ("Where Are You Going?" in *1978 Devotional Speeches of the Year: BYU Devotional and Fireside Addresses* [Provo, Utah: Brigham Young University Press, 1979], pp. 93–94.)

Clean Hands and a
Pure Heart

Psalm 24:3–5

Ancient Israel was commanded to offer up the firstlings of their flocks as a sacrifice to the Lord. While Moses led the children of Israel, these sacrifices were made in the courtyard of the portable tabernacle. But after Jesus Christ offered himself as a sacrifice for all mankind through the shedding of his blood, he commanded that animal sacrifice end. Today the sacrifice required to worthily enter the temple is that of "a broken heart and a contrite spirit." (See 3 Nephi 9:19–20.)

As the Psalmist wrote, "Who shall ascend into the hill of the Lord? or who shall stand in his holy place? He that hath clean hands, and a pure heart; who hath not lifted up his soul unto vanity, nor sworn deceitfully. He shall receive the blessing from the Lord, and righteousness from the God of his salvation." (Psalm 24:3–5.)

A Recommend for a Dollar

President John Taylor was given a blessing at Nauvoo by the Prophet Joseph Smith, in which he was told: "Elder Taylor you have now received the Holy Spirit, and if you are faithful in heeding its promptings the day will come when it will be within you a fountain of continuous revelation from God . . . so that you will know all things."

President Taylor was standing by the east pulpit on the morning of [the] dedication [of the Logan Temple], watching the hundreds of people filing into the assembly hall through the four doorways in the corners of the building. He turned to President Charles O. Card and said: "See that woman coming through the doorway. Don't let her come into the assembly. She is not worthy."

Brother Card was greatly surprised and said: "Why not? She had to have a recommend, and she had to present it at the door. Surely she is all right."

President Taylor answered: "I know not, but the Spirit of God tells me she is not worthy."

Brother Card found the woman and asked to see her recommend, which she had. She raised no opposition when he found she was not a Mormon and asked her to leave the room. She also gave him her name and address. Brother Card later visited her at her home and asked how she had obtained her recommend. The Bishop of the ward had issued a recommend to one of his inactive couples, thinking they would be so happy that they would renew their religious duties in the ward. This man met the woman on the street and asked how she would like to go to the dedication services. She said she would like to but could not get a recommend. He said: "I have a recommend and will give it to you for one dollar." She had a dollar and exchanged it for the recommend. It almost worked until the Lord spotted her and sent her out.

President Taylor did not know the woman, and had never seen her before, but he listened to the promptings of the Holy Ghost, and his spirit of discernment picked the one person in 2,000 who should not have been there. (Nolan Porter Olsen, *Logan Temple: The First 100 Years* [Providence, Utah: Keith W. Watkins and Sons, 1978], pp. 152–53.)

The Spirit of Discernment

Elder Spencer W. Kimball related the following story that had come down to his family about his grandfather Heber C. Kimball. He gave the story, he said, as it was told to him.

Being in charge of the Endowment House, while the Temple was in the process of construction, Heber C. Kimball met with a group who were planning to enter the temple for ordinance work. He felt impressed that some were not worthy to go into the temple, and he suggested first that if any present were not worthy, they might retire. No one responding, he said that there were some present who should not proceed through the temple because of unworthiness and he wished they would leave so the company could proceed. It was quiet as death and no one moved nor responded. A third time he spoke, saying that there were two people present who were in adultery, and if they did not leave he would call out their names. Two people walked out and the company continued on through the temple. (In *The Miracle of Forgiveness* [Salt Lake City: Bookcraft, 1969], p. 112.)

The Thanksgiving
Psalm

Psalm 100

"Make a joyful noise unto the Lord, all ye lands. Serve the Lord with gladness: come before his presence with singing. Know ye that the Lord he is God: it is he that hath made us, and not we ourselves; we are his people, and the sheep of his pasture. Enter into his gates with thanksgiving, and into his courts with praise: be thankful unto him, and bless his name. For the Lord is good; his mercy is everlasting; and his truth endureth to all generations." (Psalm 100:1–5.)

Chaplain B. H. Roberts

When the Utah National Guard was mustered into the regular Army shortly after the United States entered World War I, Elder B. H. Roberts, a member of the First Council of the Seventy, was also serving on reserve duty as chaplain of the 145th Field Artillery (1st Utah Battalion).

Having passed his 60th birthday, Elder Roberts was worried whether or not his physical condition would keep him from serving on active duty.

Seventeen years earlier, the U.S. Congress had denied him his seat as U.S. representative from the State of Utah, which refusal denied him the opportunity to serve his country.

Elder Roberts was a patriotic man and the congressional

refusal had been a painful experience. He was now determined to do everything possible to avoid a second denial.

Consequently, he spent many hours conditioning his body in order to pass the physical examination. Happily, he passed, and when his unit was called to active duty in August 1917, he became the first member of the Church to serve in the Chaplain's Corps of the U.S. Armed Forces.

The bitter anti-Mormon feeling of the 19th Century had not completely died out during the early 1900s. Ministers of other denominations had been ardent in their aversion to, and their denunciation of, the Mormons.

This resentment became very apparent in France during the Thanksgiving season of 1918.

The last Thursday in November fell shortly after Nov. 11, 1918, the signing of the Armistice. Everyone was grateful for the ending of hostilities and Thanksgiving Day found the American "doughboys" gathered in one grand Thanksgiving service.

The large attendance included high-ranking military officers and the services were conducted by the chaplains, who were seated on the grandstand.

Elder Roberts was relegated to one of the rear seats. He had not been asked in advance to participate on the program, therefore, it was with great surprise that he heard the chaplain in charge announce: "Elder Roberts, the Mormon chaplain from Utah, will now step up and read the Thanksgiving Psalm."

Elder Roberts had never heard of the Thanksgiving Psalm but, hiding his personal embarrassment and possible impending embarrassment to the Church, he arose and walked to the podium, not knowing what he should say.

Years later he testified that, during the long walk to the front, he distinctly heard an audible voice announce: "The 100th Psalm."

It was as clear as though another person had spoken at his side.

Elder Roberts faced the crowd, paused, then opened his Bible and read Psalm 100:

"Make a joyful noise unto the Lord, all ye lands. Serve the Lord with gladness: come before his presence with singing. Know ye that the Lord he is God: it is he that hath made us, and not we ourselves; we are his people, and the sheep of his pasture.

"Enter into his gates with thanksgiving, and into his courts with praise: be thankful unto him, and bless his name. For the Lord is good; his mercy is everlasting; and his truth endureth to all generations."

After Brother Roberts had closed his Bible and was returning to his seat, he noticed that his fellow chaplains refused to look at him; their eyes were immovably fixed on the floor.

It was then he realized that his part on the program had been a deliberate attempt to embarrass him, the Church and the priesthood. He acknowledged the help which he had received from the Lord in his moment of need and, when he returned to his tent that night, he checked the Book of Psalms, discovering that the 100th Psalm contained the most pertinent and appropriate sentiments on Thanksgiving. ("Inspiration Key to Thanksgiving Psalm," *Church News*, 22 November 1975, p. 12; see also Truman G. Madsen, *Defender of the Faith: The B. H. Roberts Story* [Salt Lake City: Bookcraft, 1980], pp. 311–12.)

Trust in the Lord

Proverbs 3:5–6

"Trust in the Lord with all thine heart; and lean not unto thine own understanding. In all thy ways acknowledge him, and he shall direct thy paths." (Proverbs 3:5–6.)

Glass for the Tabernacle

On one [television] program ["Death Valley Days"], the Old Ranger related how the glass was obtained for the windows of the St. George Tabernacle. The glass had been manufactured in the East. Then it had been placed on a ship in New York, which sailed forth on the long and at times perilous journey around Cape Horn and up to the West Coast of America. The precious glass, stored in cartons, was then transported to San Bernardino, California, to await the overland trek to St. George.

David Cannon and the brethren in St. George had the duty to go to San Bernardino with their teams and wagons to retrieve the glass, that the tabernacle of the Lord could be completed. One problem: They needed the then-astronomical sum of $800 to pay for the glass. They had no money. David Cannon turned to his wife and his son and asked, "Do you think that we can raise the money, that we might obtain the glass for the tabernacle?"

His tiny boy, David, Jr., said, "Daddy, I know we can!"

He then produced two cents of his own money and gave it to his father. Wilhelmina Cannon, David's wife, went through the secret hiding places that all women have in their houses. Her search produced $3.50 in silver. The community was scoured for money, and at length the sum of $200 was accumulated—$600 short of the required amount.

David Cannon sighed the sigh of despair of one who had failed although he had tried his best. The little family was really too weary to sleep and too discouraged to eat, so they prayed. Morning dawned. There gathered the teamsters with their wagons and teams, prepared to undertake the long journey to San Bernardino. But they had no $600.

Then there came a knock at the door, and Peter Nielsen, from the nearby community of Washington, entered the house. He said to David Cannon, "Brother David, I have had a persistent dream that I should bring the money that I had saved to expand my house—bring it to you, that you would have a purpose for it."

While all of the men gathered around the table, including little David, Jr., Peter Nielsen took out a red bandanna and dropped gold pieces, one by one, upon the table. When David Cannon counted the gold pieces, they totaled $600— the exact amount needed to obtain the glass. Within an hour the men waved good-bye and, with their teams, set forth on their journey to San Bernardino to retrieve the glass for the tabernacle. (Thomas S. Monson, "Tears, Trials, Trust, Testimony," *Ensign*, May 1987, p. 44.)

Parable of the Unwise Bee

Sometimes I find myself under obligations of work requiring quiet and seclusion such as neither my comfortable office nor the cozy study at home insures. My favorite retreat is an upper room in the tower of a large building, well removed from the noise and confusion of the city streets. The room is somewhat difficult of access, and relatively secure against human intrusion. Therein I have spent many peaceful and busy hours with books and pen.

I am not always without visitors, however, especially in

summertime; for, when I sit with windows open, flying insects occasionally find entrance and share the place with me. These self-invited guests are not unwelcome. Many a time I have laid down the pen and, forgetful of my theme, have watched with interest the activities of these winged visitants, with an afterthought that the time so spent had not been wasted, for, is it not true, that even a butterfly, a beetle, or a bee, may be a bearer of lessons to the receptive student?

A wild bee from the neighboring hills once flew into the room; and at intervals during an hour or more I caught the pleasing hum of its flight. The little creature realized that it was a prisoner, yet all its efforts to find the exit through the partly opened casement failed. When ready to close up the room and leave, I threw the window wide, and tried at first to guide and then to drive the bee to liberty and safety, knowing well that if left in the room it would die as other insects there entrapped had perished in the dry atmosphere of the enclosure. The more I tried to drive it out, the more determinedly did it oppose and resist my efforts. Its erstwhile peaceful hum developed into an angry roar, its darting flight became hostile and threatening.

Then it caught me off my guard and stung my hand—the hand that would have guided it to freedom. At last it alighted on a pendant attached to the ceiling, beyond my reach of help or injury. The sharp pain of its unkind sting aroused in me rather pity than anger. I knew the inevitable penalty of its mistaken opposition and defiance; and I had to leave the creature to its fate. Three days later I returned to the room and found the dried, lifeless body of the bee on the writing table. It had paid for its stubbornness with its life.

To the bee's short-sightedness and selfish misunderstanding I was a foe, a persistent persecutor, a mortal enemy bent on its destruction; while in truth I was its friend, offering it ransom of the life it had put in forfeit through its own error, striving to redeem it, in spite of itself, from the prison-house of death and restore it to the outer air of liberty.

Are we so much wiser than the bee that no analogy lies between its unwise course and our lives? We are prone to contend, sometimes with vehemence and anger, against the adversity which after all may be the manifestation of superior

wisdom and loving care, directed against our temporary comfort for our permanent blessing. In the tribulations and suffer-
ings of mortality there is a divine ministry which only the
godless soul can wholly fail to discern. To many the loss of
wealth has been a boon, a providential means of leading or
driving them from the confines of selfish indulgence to the
sunshine and the open, where boundless opportunity waits
on effort. Disappointment, sorrow, and affliction may be the
expression of an all-wise Father's kindness.

Consider the lesson of the unwise bee!

"Trust in the Lord with all thine heart; and lean not
unto thine own understanding.

"In all thy ways acknowledge him, and he shall direct
thy paths." (Proverbs 3:5–6.) (James E. Talmage, "The
Parable of the Unwise Bee," *Improvement Era,* November
1962, p. 817.)

A True Friend

Proverbs 17:9

"He that covereth a transgression seeketh love; but he that repeateth a matter separateth very friends" (Proverbs 17:9).

Alan and Robbie

Alan was the only member of the Church in his third-grade class. Robbie, who sat next to Alan, was having a particularly hard day. He could not seem to control his enthusiasm. During the science experiment after lunch, he did not stay in his seat and talked out of turn. Finally, Mrs. Wakefield became so irritated that she wrote his name on the chalkboard. The class grew very quiet. Everyone knew that Robbie would have to meet after school with the principal, and that his parents would be called.

With fifteen minutes remaining in the school day, Mrs. Wakefield took an opportunity, as she often did on Friday, to reward a student who had achieved well during the week. Today she selected Alan. She stood by his desk and reviewed with the students the many good things he had accomplished that week.

Usually the chosen student received a piece of candy or a pencil from among the prizes that Mrs. Wakefield kept in her desk drawer. As she offered Alan the opportunity to choose his prize, classmates began to offer their advice. "Ask for a *Star Wars* eraser." "Go for the candy bar." And a final recommendation: "See if she will let you leave class ten minutes early."

Instead of heeding his classmates, Alan stood and made his way to the chalkboard. As everyone watched, and with Mrs. Wakefield's permission, he erased Robbie's name. (Ron R. Munns, "True Friends—True to the Faith," *Ensign*, October 1992, pp. 19–20.)

Cast Thy Bread upon
the Waters

Ecclesiastes 11:1

"Cast thy bread upon the waters: for thou shalt find it after many days" (Ecclesiastes 11:1).

Milk Day

Among the many wonderful people we met when we lived in a small town in Utah years ago was a family named Williams. They were a good family of strong faith and testimony. But Brother and Sister Williams had five small children and struggled to make ends meet. Then Brother Williams' back was broken in an automobile accident, and he was hospitalized for several weeks.

As counselor in our ward Relief Society presidency, I went with our president to visit Sister Williams and her young family. What a blessing the Church welfare program is at a time like this! As our president explained how the program worked, Sister Williams was relieved of many anxieties.

When I arrived home, I couldn't get the plight of this young mother out of my mind. I could identify with her because we had six young children at home, and they really kept me busy. I kept wondering what I personally could do for her. My thoughts went to milk. I was sure her family drank milk by the gallons, as mine did, and we had found a dairy that sold milk cheaper than the stores or home delivery. I called Sister Williams about it, and she told me she got her milk there too, so I arranged to get hers when I went for mine. When I went to pick up her cans, she had them and the money ready for me, but I told her I would like to buy her milk that day. She resisted, but finally relented.

I went back a couple of days later to get her cans again, but she was hesitant—she didn't have any money. I told her not to worry, that I wanted to buy the milk for her. This arrangment went on for several weeks, until I began to feel the strain on my own budget and found myself borrowing money from my children.

But just as I decided I would have to tell Sister Williams that I could no longer buy her milk, I noticed that every "milk day" some little miracle would happen. I remember one day there simply was no extra money and I was ready to reach for the phone when I was prompted to go to the mailbox first. I did; and there was a little check—just enough for the milk—for some jury duty I had performed earlier in the year. I continued to buy milk.

One evening several weeks later Brother Williams was released from the hospital. He was in a brace, but he insisted on coming by our home to thank us personally for buying their milk. However, their compensation checks were coming in now, and everything was going to be all right for them.

After they left, I leaned against the door and silently thanked the Lord that I had never told Sister Williams I couldn't get her milk. Still, that very day I had only had enough money to buy their milk, but not ours; and our littlest, Chuck, would be awake at six o'clock next morning, wanting a drink.

The very next morning, before Chuck was even awake, there came a knock on our door. On the step stood a young man from our ward holding two big jugs of milk. He said, "Sister Cutler, I understand you have a big family. For some reason or other our cow has started giving more milk than we can use, and we just hate pouring it down the sink. Would you be insulted if I dropped it off here each morning on my way to work?"

I couldn't believe it! Immediately, into my mind flashed

a saying I had heard my mother quote often when I was a little girl: "Cast your bread upon the waters, and after many days it will return—buttered" (Ecclesiastes 11:1). By the time that cow got back to normal production, we had received two or three times more milk than we had ever given away. (Carma N. Cutler, "Cast Your Bread . . . ," *Ensign*, June 1981, pp. 70–71.)

Call the Sabbath
a Delight

Isaiah 58:13–14

"If thou turn away thy foot from the sabbath, from doing thy pleasure on my holy day; and call the sabbath a delight, the holy of the Lord, honourable; and shalt honour him, not doing thine own ways, nor finding thine own pleasure, nor speaking thine own words: then shalt thou delight thyself in the Lord; and I will cause thee to ride upon the high places of the earth, and feed thee with the heritage of Jacob thy Father: for the mouth of the Lord hath spoken it" (Isaiah 58:13–14).

Not Open on Sunday

"If you took a look at my books, you might not be quite so anxious to open your store on Sunday! I can show you mathematically that we did not make any profit on Sunday during the years our business was open on Sunday!"

As a young couple, my wife and I worked for several years in Idaho Falls in eating establishments which were open on Sunday. During that time, we noticed that on Sunday, the business often lost money. The machinery always seemed to break down, and then we could not serve the customers. Repairmen charged twice as much on that day. Good hired help was hard to find. We vowed that if we were ever able to buy a business of our own, we would make some changes.

The opportunity finally came one year with the purchase

of a drive-in. The loan we took out to buy the business was heavy, and the finance people and the owners of surrounding food establishments assured us that we did not have the slightest chance of paying off our loan if we did not compete on the biggest sales day of the week—Sunday. Because we had already paid the down payment and wanted to make a success of our enterprise we felt trapped. We stayed open.

As predicted, Sunday proved to be our biggest day. Having made the decision to stay open on Sunday, we couldn't change. We were afraid of the business we would lose. Eventually, in the back of our minds, grew the fear that if we did not serve people on Sunday, we would lose our customers and be unable to raise the more than $60,000 we needed to make the business ours.

We had almost reached our goal when I had a heart attack. Because good Sunday help was hard to find, we agreed to close on Sunday from Thanksgiving until Father's Day.

My doctor was pleased with our decision, happy that I could get some much needed rest. But as the months passed, I became worried about the low volume of business we had on our books. One day I told my wife that we should again open on Sunday. She looked at me in silence for several seconds, then said, "First, go look in the mirror and see if you look like a man who could stand seven days of work each week!"

"I guess I don't have to look," I answered slowly. "We'd better forget the whole idea."

Later, as we sat down together to review and evaluate our business year, our fears were confirmed—our gross sales were over $17,000 lower than the previous years! But in spite of our low volume, our balance showed only $10.00 less profit! We were amazed. Pleased with such figures, we agreed to keep the drive-in closed on Sunday for another year. Again, the volume was way down but the profit was no less. Our drive-in was a success without opening on Sunday!

When I think of the poor effect on my health and all the work I did for *nothing* on those Sundays, I am surprised it took me as long to learn the lesson that obedience to the law of the Sabbath carries its own reward. The Sabbath is the Lord's day. We will all be blessed for honoring it. (Quinten and LaRae Warr, as told to Ruth Heiner, "Not Open on Sunday!" *Ensign,* June 1984, pp. 63–64.)

Children's Teeth
Set on Edge

Jeremiah 31:29–30

"In those days they shall say no more, The fathers have eaten a sour grape, and the children's teeth are set on edge. But every one shall die for his own iniquity: every man that eateth the sour grape, his teeth shall be set on edge." (Jeremiah 31:29–30.)

Sour Grapes! Such Unhappy Food!

There is the man who resisted release from positions in the Church. He knew positions were temporary trusts, but he criticized the presiding leader who had released him, complaining that proper recognition had not been given; the time had not been propitious; it had been a reflection upon his effectiveness. He bitterly built up a case for himself, absented himself from his meetings, and justified himself in his resultant estrangement. His children partook of his frustrations, and his children's children. In later life he "came to himself," and on the brink of the grave made an about-face. His family would not effect the transformation which now he would give his life to have them make. How selfish! Haughty pride induces eating sour grapes, and innocent ones have their teeth set on edge. . . .

When I was a child, we used the expression, "He cut off his nose to spite his face." To us, that meant that one was fighting against fate, rebelling against the inevitable, damaging himself to spite others, breaking his toe to give vent to his senseless anger.

Eight lovely children had blessed the temple marriage of a man and woman who in later years were denied a temple recommend. They would not be so dealt with by this young bishop. Why should they be deprived and humiliated? Were they less worthy than others? They argued that this boy-bishop was too strict, too orthodox. Never would they be active, nor enter the door of that Church as long as that bishop presided. They would show him. The history of this family is tragic. The four younger ones were never baptized; the four older ones never were ordained, endowed, nor sealed. No missions were filled by this family. Today the parents are ill at ease, still defiant. They had covered themselves with a cloud, and righteous prayers could not pass through (see Lamentations 3:44).

Sour grapes! Such unhappy food! (Spencer W. Kimball, in Conference Report, April 1955, p. 95.)

But If Not . . .

Daniel 3:1–18

King Nebuchadnezzar created a ninety-foot golden image of himself and commanded every one in Babylon to fall down and worship it immediately when the trumpets sounded. Three Israeli boys, Shadrach, Meshach, and Abed-nego, refused to bow before King Nebuchadnezzar's golden image. They were arrested and sentenced to die in a fiery furnace. As they stood before the king they said with great faith, "If it be so, our God whom we serve is able to deliver us from the burning fiery furnace, and he will deliver us out of thine hand, O king. But if not, be it known unto thee, O king, that we will not serve thy gods, nor worship the golden image which thou hast set up." (See Daniel 3:1–18.)

These three were courageous not because God delivered them but because whether he delivered them or not they were not going to break the Lord's commandments by worshipping false idols. When they stood before the king they had no assurance that they would escape unharmed. Three young women in the book of Abraham who faced a similar situation were not so fortunate. They lost their lives because they refused to worship the immoral gods of the Egyptians. (See Abraham 1:11.)

Youth today will need that kind of courage to be able to stand up for principles and values, not because they think they might be blessed for doing so, but because they hold these values so deeply that they refuse to violate them.

The Courage of David Opont

On 7 March 1990, the day before he was to turn twelve, eleven-year-old David Opont was walking with his friends to school in New York City. A thirteen-year-old bully—who apparently had robbed David the day before—cornered David, dragged him into a nearby garage, and ordered him to smoke crack. David refused, and the bully tied him to a railing and beat him with a baseball bat. The bully demanded that David do the drugs or he would be set on fire. Upon David's refusal, the bully set the eleven-year-old aflame. David received second- and third-degree burns over 55 percent of his body. Friends took him to the hospital. When he arrived the doctors gave him a 50-50 chance to live.

While recovering from surgery, David received birthday wishes from former president Ronald Reagan and New York City mayor David Dinkins. Other well-wishers included actor Bill Cosby and Vice President Dan Quayle.

An article appearing in the *Deseret News* three months later reported that on Friday, 8 June 1990, "David Opont rose from his wheelchair, smiled shyly and said he felt fine as he left [the] hospital." The newspaper article went on to say:

> With the spirit that marked his remarkable recovery, he faced dozens of television cameras and reporters on the lawn of The York Hospital-Cornell Medical Center and said, "I have to thank God, my doctors and nurses.
> "The first thing I want to do is go to school," he said.
> Asked how he felt, the boy said in a soft voice: "Fine."
> David then was wheeled to an ambulance that took him to a helicopter for transit to the Margaret T. Palomino Rehabilitation Center at Jamaica Hospital. There he will undergo physical therapy and reconstructive surgery, mostly cosmetic, and receive counseling for the next three to four weeks, doctors said.

The thirteen-year-old bully was arrested hours after the attack on David and was jailed at a juvenile center. He was charged with attempted murder, assault, kidnapping, robbery, and attempted robbery. (See "Burn Victim Leaves Hospital with Smile and Thank-you," *Deseret News*, 9 June 1990, p. A3. See also "Bully's Victim Undergoes Skin-graft Operation," *Deseret News*, 10 March 1990, p. A4; "Reagan, Dinkins Send Wishes to N.Y. Boy, 12, Set Afire for Not Smoking Crack," *Jet*, 26 March 1990, p. 55.)

The Writing on the Wall

Daniel 5:1-17

Belshazzar the king made a great feast to a thousand of his lords, and drank wine before the thousand. . . .

Then they brought the golden vessels that were taken out of the temple of the house of God which was at Jerusalem; and the king, and his princes, his wives, and his concubines, drank in them.

They drank wine, and praised the gods of gold, and of silver, of brass, of iron, of wood, and of stone.

In the same hour came forth fingers of a man's hand, and wrote over against the candlestick upon the plaister of the wall of the king's palace: and the king saw the part of the hand that wrote. . . .

. . . And the king spake, and said to the wise men of Babylon, Whosoever shall read this writing, and shew me the interpretation thereof, shall be clothed with scarlet, and have a chain of gold about his neck. . . .

. . . And the queen spake and said, . . .

There is a man in thy kingdom, in whom is the spirit of the holy gods. . . .

. . . Let Daniel be called, and he will shew the interpretation.

Then was Daniel brought in before the king. . . .

Then Daniel answered . . . I will read the writing unto the king, and make known to him the interpretation. (Daniel 5:1, 3–5, 7, 10, 11, 12–13, 17.)

A Missionary Miracle

In the Spring of 1856, in the days of my youth, I was called by the First Presidency of the Church . . . to go on a mission to Australia, to preach the gospel. I was young and inexperienced, and had but very little education. I had been to school but six months in my life. . . . The scriptures I never had read, from the fact that I could not read. Under these circumstances I went to President Heber C. Kimball and asked permission to stay at home one year, and I would go to school and learn to read and write, and then I would go. But he said that he had called me to a mission and he wanted me to go now. I received my endowments, and President Kimball blessed me and prophesied many great things . . . ; for he said that I . . . should learn to read and write by my close application and the help of the Holy Spirit. . . .

We arrived at San Francisco and there was a ship about to sail for Australia. . . . In thirty-six days we arrived at Sydney, Australia, having sailed about 10,000 miles and had a pleasant voyage. . . .

We . . . went to a city called Picton. . . . We applied for the court-house and obtained it from the judge of the district. We appointed a meeting for Friday evening. . . . At the time appointed the people assembled and filled the house. For two days my companion had been marking passages in the Bible, and on this occasion he was intending to deliver a fine discourse. The meeting was opened and he arose, took his text and commenced with great importance. He had not spoken more than five minutes when he got to the end of his sermon, for he could not say more than "Amen." Then I was introduced to the congregation as Elder Potter, with the remark that I would continue the subject of the gospel. I arose with fear and trembling; for it was the first time in my life that I had stood in a pulpit. Before me was a large Bible and prayer book. I must say that my mind was confused; but I took a text from the Bible that lay open before me. It was from the Prophet Amos:

"Surely the Lord God will do nothing, but He revealeth His secret unto His servants the prophets."

After reading it I spoke a few more words and became

dumb that I could not speak. I stood there without speaking about two minutes, when the words of President Heber C. Kimball came to me: He said that the time would come when I should be at a loss to know what to say to the people, "and, at that time," he said, "if you will commence to declare the divine mission of Joseph Smith in this our day, and the divine authenticity of the Book of Mormon, the Lord will loosen your tongue and you shall say the very things that are needful to be said to the people." When this came to my mind I commenced declaring these things to the congregation. I had spoken but a few minutes, when I thought I saw several lines of large letters printed on the walls of the house, and I commenced to read them and spoke about one hour. When the letters faded from my sight I then stopped speaking. I could not tell all that I had said; but my companion told me it was an excellent discourse. (Amasa Potter, "The Lord's Blessings," in *Labors in the Vineyard* [Salt Lake City: Juvenile Instructor Office, 1884], pp. 75–76, 78–79. *Labors in the Vineyard* was reprinted as part of the 4-vols.-in-1 publication *Classic Experiences and Adventures* [Salt Lake City: Bookcraft, 1969].)

Putting the First Commandment First

Daniel 6

Even while living as an exile in Babylon, Daniel remembered the first commandment, "Thou shalt have no other gods before me," and was blessed by the Lord. King Darius of Babylon was so impressed with Daniel that he promoted him to be the first of all his presidents. Jealousy and covetousness led the other presidents and princes to seek to "find occasion against Daniel." But they could not do so, because "he was faithful, neither was there any error or fault found in him."

Knowing that Daniel prayed three times a day to God, they formed a secret combination and conspired against him by appealing to King Darius's vanity. They persuaded the king to issue a decree that anyone who prayed to any god or man for thirty days, except to King Darius, would "be cast into the den of lions."

The record states: "Now when Daniel knew that the writing was signed, he went into his house; and his windows being open in his chamber toward Jerusalem, he kneeled upon his knees three times a day, and prayed, and gave thanks before his God, as he did aforetime."

The wicked men gathered together and saw Daniel praying. They immediately rushed to the king. "Hast thou not signed a decree, that every man that shall ask a petition of any God or man within thirty days, save of thee, O king, shall be cast into the den of lions? The king answered and said, The thing is true, according to the law of the Medes and Persians, which altereth not."

Then they answered and said that Daniel had broken the unalterable law and that in fact he was praying to his God three times a day. "Then the king, when he heard these words, was sore displeased with himself, and set his heart on Daniel to deliver him: and he laboured till the going down of the sun to deliver him."

But later that evening, the men assembled before the king and said, "Know, O king, that the law of the Medes and Persians is, That no decree nor statute which the king establisheth may be changed." (See Daniel 6:1–15.)

The biblical record relates what happened next:

> Then the king commanded, and they brought Daniel, and cast him into the den of lions. Now the king spake and said unto Daniel, Thy God whom thou servest continually, he will deliver thee.
>
> And a stone was brought, and laid upon the mouth of the den; and the king sealed it with his own signet, and with the signet of his lords; that the purpose might not be changed concerning Daniel.
>
> Then the king went to his palace, and passed the night fasting: neither were instruments of musick brought before him: and his sleep went from him.
>
> Then the king arose very early in the morning, and went in haste unto the den of lions.
>
> And when he came to the den, he cried with a lamentable voice unto Daniel: and the king spake and said to Daniel, O Daniel, servant of the living God, is thy God, whom thou servest continually, able to deliver thee from the lions?
>
> Then said Daniel unto the king, O king, live for ever.
>
> My God hath sent his angel, and hath shut the lions' mouths, that they have not hurt me: forasmuch as before him innocency was found in me; and also before thee, O king, have I done no hurt.
>
> Then was the king exceeding glad for him, and commanded that they should take Daniel up out of the den. So

Daniel was taken up out of the den, and no manner of hurt was found upon him, because he believed in his God.

And the king commanded, and they brought those men which had accused Daniel, and they cast them into the den of lions, them, their children, and their wives; and the lions had the mastery of them, and brake all their bones in pieces or ever they came at the bottom of the den. (Daniel 6:16–24.)

The Freedom to Pray

The *Deseret News* of 8 June 1991 reported the following:

A Bingham High School student leader offered a prayer at his graduation ceremony Thursday night, despite a Jordan School District ban on prayers at commencements.

"They told me not to say a prayer. But that's a crock," said Josh Peterson, 17. "I've been thinking about it since last year. It took me a while, but I just finally decided you've got to do what you think is right.

"I didn't mean to hurt anyone's feelings, but I'm not sorry for what I did. It's tradition, for crying out loud." . . .

The constitutionality of prayers at high school graduations is expected to be argued before the U.S. Supreme Court this fall. The Jordan District board, seeking to avoid the cost of litigation, banned graduation prayer in 1989 after two Brighton High students sued over the issue.

Peterson, who served this past school year as Bingham High student body president, said he submitted to the school's graduation advisers a copy of reflective comments he was scheduled to deliver during the commencement.

He knew he might depart from the text to say the prayer. But it wasn't until shortly before he started talking that he decided to actually go through with it, he said.

"I said this, 'If I could say a prayer, this is what I would say,'" Peterson said. Then he delivered what observers called a traditional LDS Church prayer.

"I was a little nervous. But then I prayed about it," he said.

The audience was shocked at first. But after senior class president Brandon Julio pronounced the prayer "awesome," the crowd gave a standing ovation, said Kevin Thompson, one of Bingham's two valedictorians. . . .

Peterson said he doesn't want to be made out a hero, but if he had the chance to do it all over again, he would say the prayer.

"Oh, definitely," Peterson said. "I think prayer is a special case in that it's tradition, and that is what our country was founded on." (Patty Henetz, "Bingham Student Defies Ban, Gives Graduation Prayer," *Deseret News*, 8 June 1991, pp. A1, A2.)

The main parallel we can observe between these two stories is the assertion of a principle—the freedom to pray to God. There will be different opinions about the advisability of Josh Peterson's actions, and certainly not everybody who believes in religious freedom would choose to make this kind of protest. But this story is included as a modern affirmation of an age-old principle.

Saviors on Mount Zion

Obadiah 1:21

"And saviours shall come up on mount Zion to judge the mount of Esau; and the kingdom shall be the Lord's" (Obadiah 1:21).

Blessed in the St. George Temple

A few weeks before I turned eight years old, my father was killed in a trucking accident. A month later, we moved to a new home in St. George, Utah, across the street from the large vacant field just east of the beautiful white temple.

Mother was soon called to be the stake genealogy secretary. Whenever a group assigned could not make it, a member of the temple presidency would call mother to ask if her sons could come to the temple to do baptisms for the dead. Mother never turned the Lord down. My two older brothers and I often went to the temple to do baptisms.

One summer's day, I had cut my hand severely on an empty can. I begged Mother not to take me for stitches, so she cleaned the wound, applied a "butterfly" bandage, covered that with a band-aid, and then wrapped my hand in gauze.

No sooner had she finished than the telephone rang. It was the brethren from the temple, wanting us boys to come over to do baptisms. Because my two older brothers had been very busy lately, I had been going to the temple on a regular basis. I had by now compiled a lengthy list of baptisms for the dead that ran into thousands. Once again, my older brothers were not around, so I hurriedly bathed, dressed, and ran over to the temple.

Several hours and four hundred names later, Brother Edwards and I stopped for the night. I remember him well, his right arm to the square revealing a hand missing most of the fingers because of an accident he had had in his youth. After every baptism, he would carefully help me up into the stainless steel chair, where I was confirmed. After every twenty or thirty baptisms, Brother Edwards would look down at me and say, "Brother Fish, can you do some more?" I would answer yes, and away we would go.

As I drifted through the back door, exhausted, Mother spotted the dripping gauze on my hand and helped me into the bathroom to re-dress the wound. So tired and hungry that I just wanted to eat and sleep, I wasn't paying attention to my hand. I let her unwrap the bandage.

The gauze came off first, then the band-aid, and finally the butterfly bandage. My mother looked shocked. I looked down. Not a trace of a cut remained—no scar, no redness, nothing!

I remember my mother quietly hugging me. As we cried together, sharing that moment, the Spirit bore witness to me that I had been healed because of my service in the temple of the Lord. (Jon B. Fish, "After Four Hundred Names . . . ," *Ensign,* February 1986, p. 58.)

Jonah's Missionary Call

Jonah 1:1–17

Now the word of the Lord came unto Jonah the son of Amittai, saying,

Arise, go to Nineveh, that great city, and cry against it; for their wickedness is come up before me.

But Jonah rose up to flee unto Tarshish from the presence of the Lord, and went down to Joppa; and he found a ship going to Tarshish. . . .

But the Lord sent out a great wind into the sea, and there was a mighty tempest in the sea, so that the ship was like to be broken. . . .

And they said every one to his fellow, Come, and let us cast lots, that we may know for whose cause this evil is upon us. So they cast lots, and the lot fell upon Jonah. . . .

And he said unto them, I am an Hebrew; and I fear the Lord. . . .

Then were the men exceedingly afraid, and said unto him, Why hast thou done this? For the men knew that he fled from the presence of the Lord. . . .

And he said unto them, Take me up, and cast me forth into the sea; so shall the sea be calm unto you: for I know that for my sake this great tempest is upon you. . . .

So they took up Jonah, and cast him forth into the sea. . . .

Now the Lord had prepared a great fish to swallow up

Jonah. And Jonah was in the belly of the fish three days and three nights. (Jonah 1:1–4, 7, 9–10, 12, 15, 17.)

Memory of a Determined Missionary

Elder Joe J. Christensen shared the following account of one Church member's experience relative to full-time missionary service:

A few years ago, while serving as president of the Missionary Training Center in Provo, Utah, I had a delightful visit with one of the missionaries who came into my office. He was obviously older than the average young elder. He was about twenty-five years of age. He told me of his conversion.

When he was sixteen, he was baptized into the Church in Europe along with his mother. His father did not object to his wife's and son's joining the Church, even though he was not interested. He was a banker and wanted his son to prepare himself for a profession in the same area.

The young man loved studying the scriptures, but occasionally had some difficulty when his father would interrupt him when he was studying his seminary course and say, "Don't waste your time studying those things. Study your regular school courses so that you can be accepted at the university."

The elder said, "One night later on, when I was about eighteen, I had a dream. I dreamed that I had been called on a mission to Japan. I felt so good about it. I really wanted to go. The next day, when I told my parents about my dream, my dad strongly objected. He said, 'Oh, no! Don't waste two years of your life on a mission. You need to get on with your university studies.'"

Since he was too young to leave for a mission at that time anyway, he did go on with his university studies. He chose to come to Brigham Young University. He majored in finance and banking for his undergraduate degree and stayed to complete a master's degree in business administration.

He was hired by an international banking firm in

Germany and was doing very well as a promising junior executive, but the idea of filling a mission would not leave his mind, and so he went to visit with his bishop and stake president. When he told his stake president of the vivid dream he had years before about going on a mission to Japan, his stake president chuckled and said, "Well, I don't think you will be going to Japan. Missionaries from here generally are called to some other country on the continent, and a few go over to the British Isles."

When he received his call and his father heard of it, he came and tried to change his son's mind because he thought that a two-year interruption would be a disaster for his son's professional career. One of the bank executives came down from Frankfurt and tried to discourage him from leaving, saying something like, "My boy, do you know how much this will cost you in salary and opportunity loss? You ought to sit down and figure it out."

The elder said that he did that, and he had determined that the mission would cost him a very large amount of money—more than 150,000 dollars. Then tears came to his eyes, and he said, "But President, if it were to cost several times that amount, I would still be here, because I know that serving a mission is what the Lord wants me to do."

That elder was one of the few I remember who left the Missionary Training Center speaking what Japanese he had learned with a German accent. He was called to Japan. He served a successful mission, and I am confident that when he finished, he found many international businesses that would like to hire a junior executive who can speak English, German, and Japanese—the major languages of the economic free world. Even if he didn't earn an extra cent, he still knew that he had done what the Lord wanted him to do. (Joe J. Christensen, "Good Memories Are Real Blessings," *Ensign*, November 1989, pp. 43–44.)

Do Justly, Love Mercy, Walk Humbly

Micah 6:7–8

In spite of the Lord's many blessings to them, ancient Israel failed to serve him in spirit and truth. They felt that if they gave of their substance rather than their hearts they would be justified. But the prophet Micah taught: "Will the Lord be pleased with thousands of rams, or with ten thousands of rivers of oil? shall I give my firstborn for my transgression, the fruit of my body for the sin of my soul? He hath shewed thee, O man, what is good; and what doth the Lord require of thee, but to do justly, and to love mercy, and to walk humbly with thy God?" (Micah 6:7–8.)

We Have an Agreement

Elder Spencer J. Condie gave the following account of a story related by Elder L. Lionel Kendrick:

> In the Philippines there is a good and faithful member of the Church who is a fisherman. Each day he makes his catch and then brings the fish to the open fish market for sale. His prices are invariably much, much lower than his competitors', and when asked why he does not raise his prices to be in line with those of the other fishermen, he humbly replied:

"The members of the Church and my neighbors all buy their fish from me. If I raised my prices to match the other fishermen's, many of them could not afford to eat fish." And then he added with a twinkle in his eye, "I have an agreement with the Lord: I help take care of his poor, and he provides me with fish. There are days when the other fishermen come back with their boats empty, but the Lord makes sure I always return with a good catch!" (Spencer J. Condie, *In Perfect Balance* [Salt Lake City: Bookcraft, 1993], p. 143.)

The Lord Will Protect Jerusalem

Zechariah 12:2, 8–9

"Behold, I will make Jerusalem a cup of trembling unto all the people round about, when they shall be in the siege both against Judah and against Jerusalem. . . . In that day shall the Lord defend the inhabitants of Jerusalem; and he that is feeble among them at that day shall be as David; and the house of David shall be as God, as the angel of the Lord before them. And it shall come to pass in that day, that I will seek to destroy all the nations that come against Jerusalem." (Zechariah 12:2, 8–9.)

The Lord Fights Modern Battles

Although the preceding scripture refers to the protection that the inhabitants of Jerusalem will receive near the end of the battle of Armageddon, the Lord has helped Jerusalem in other times of need. In this connection, Elder LeGrand Richards quoted a September 1950 article written by a man who had recently visited Palestine:

It was marvelous what God did for the Jews, especially in Jerusalem, during the fighting with the Arabs. Though quite a few months had passed since the victory of Israel's army in Israel, they were still talking about what had taken place.

Everywhere I went I heard how God had intervened in their behalf, and how He helped them to win the battles. One of the officials told me how much the Jews had to suffer. They had hardly anything with which to resist the heavy attacks of the Arabs, who were well organized and equipped with the latest weapons. Besides, they had neither food nor water because all their supplies were cut off.

The Arabs, who had a great army in strong position, were determined to destroy the Jews, while the Jews were few in number, without any arms and ammunition. The two or three guns they possessed had to be rushed from one point to another, to give the Arabs the impression that they had many of them. The Jews had quite a few tin cans which they beat as they shot the guns, giving the impression of many shots. But as the pressure was too great, they were unable to hold the lines any longer and finally decided to give up the city. At this critical moment God showed them that He was on their side, for He performed one of the greatest miracles that ever happened. The Arabs suddenly threw down their arms and surrendered. When their delegation appeared with the white flag, they asked, "Where are the three men that led you, and where are all the troops we saw?" The Jews told them that they did not know anything of the three men, for this group was their entire force. *The Arabs said that they saw three persons with long beards and flowing white robes, who warned them not to fight any longer, otherwise they would all be killed.* They became so frightened that they decided to give up. What an encouragement this was for the Jews, who realized that God was fighting for them. (Arthur U. Michelson, quoted in LeGrand Richards, *Israel! Do You Know?* [Salt Lake City: Deseret Book Co., 1954], p. 230.)

When will there be peace in the Middle East? When will the Arab and Jewish nations be restored to their homeland in Palestine in peace? The Book of Mormon declares it will happen when they believe in Christ and accept his restored gospel (see 1 Nephi 22:11–12; 2 Nephi 6:9–11; 9:1–2; 10:7; 25:15–18; 3 Nephi 16:3–4; 20:29–34).

Law of the Tithe

Malachi 3:10–12

"Bring ye all the tithes into the storehouse, that there may be meat in mine house, and prove me now herewith, saith the Lord of hosts, if I will not open you the windows of heaven, and pour you out a blessing, that there shall not be room enough to receive it. And I will rebuke the devourer for your sakes, and he shall not destroy the fruits of your ground; neither shall your vine cast her fruit before the time in the field, saith the Lord of hosts. And all nations shall call you blessed: for ye shall be a delightsome land, saith the Lord of hosts." (Malachi 3:10–12.)

Strawberry Season

During the depression years in the 1930s, we lived on a substandard farm in New Jersey, with unproductive soil yielding meager crops. Strawberries were the only plants that responded adequately to our efforts, but the strawberry season is relatively short and our yearly income was almost negligible.

I sold our strawberries in quart baskets in front of our house, which was on a county road. The returns for the strawberry season came to $40, the only ready cash we had seen for a long time. The $4 seemed a pathetically small sum to offer as tithing, and with a family of four young children, the money was desperately needed in many ways. But I was determined to pay our tithing, and did so.

We were not aware of any immediate blessings, other than having the satisfaction of doing what is right. However, the following year the strawberry-leaf blight struck the area. All the plants in the fields literally died—all but ours. Our plants remained healthy and yielded a crop of big, juicy strawberries.

People came from miles in every direction to buy our strawberries. Our customers supposed we had a hardier species and wanted to buy some of our plants for their gardens. When we told them ours were the same type they already had in their fields, they believed we must have given our strawberry patch some special attention and were skeptical when told the plants received only ordinary care. We did tell them that we had tithed our income of the previous year, but there were few Latter-day Saints in our area and most people looked askance at the mention of tithing.

Blessings may not always be so strikingly apparent. Latter-day Saints may enjoy a continuity of business success or employment and good health, and they may be inclined to take their blessings for granted, but at a time when the economy was at low ebb, our blessing of a good crop was to us an irrefutable example of the blessings that come from paying tithing. (Louise A. Kelly, "Divine Law of the Tithe," *Ensign*, June 1981, p. 69.)

Turning the Hearts of Children to Their Fathers

Malachi 4:5–6

"Behold, I will send you Elijah the prophet before the coming of the great and dreadful day of the Lord: and he shall turn the heart of the fathers to the children, and the heart of the children to their fathers, lest I come and smite the earth with a curse" (Malachi 4:5–6).

Modern Inventions Revealed to Assist the Spirit of Elijah

Christians, Jews, and Latter-day Saints all know of Malachi's prophecy and look for its fulfillment. Each Passover the Jewish people set an extra place at the seder table for the prophet Elijah. At a certain point in the Passover meal, they raise a cup of wine, open the door, and bid the prophet Elijah welcome. On 3 April 1936, during Passover, Elijah did return to the earth, just as Malachi prophesied. He didn't come to a home, however, but he appeared in the first temple built in this dispensation at Kirtland, Ohio.

When he made his appearance to the Prophet Joseph Smith and Oliver Cowdery, Elijah said: "Behold, the time has fully come, which was spoken of by the mouth of Malachi—testifying that he [Elijah] should be sent, before the great and dreadful day of the Lord come—to turn the hearts of the fathers to the children, and the children to the fathers, lest the whole earth be smitten with a curse—therefore, the keys of this dispensation are committed into your hands; and by this ye may know that the great and dreadful day of the Lord is near, even at the doors" (D&C 110:14–16).

In the April 1959 general conference, Elder Eldred G. Smith declared:

> In addition to the testimony of Joseph Smith and Oliver Cowdery, and others currently, we have factual evidence that Elijah came. One year after Elijah's coming, in 1837, laws were passed in Great Britain compelling the preservation of duplicate records of the dead. In the 400 years preceding the coming of Elijah, there were catalogued by Mr. T. B. Thompson 192 British family histories. In just one hundred years after the coming of Elijah in 1836, there were 1,879 British family histories published. . . .
>
> In 1844, just eight years after the coming of Elijah, . . . the first organization for the purpose of the gathering together records of the dead, and compiling genealogical records, was formed in the city of Boston, Massachusetts—The New England Historical and Genealogical Society.
>
> In 1869 The New York Genealogical and Biographical Society was organized. Since then literally hundreds of genealogical organizations have been organized all through the Atlantic Coast states and spreading all over Europe and the United States. (In Conference Report, April 1959, p. 99.)

On 13 November 1894 the Genealogical Society of Utah was founded to collect, compile, establish, and maintain a genealogical library for the benefit of all.

When the society was organized, Apostle Franklin D. Richards was named president. Among the first members of the board were such well-known pioneers as Wilford Woodruff, George Q. Cannon, Lorenzo Snow, and Joseph F. Smith.

In August 1987 the library's name was changed from Genealogical Library to Family History Library. Its rapid, continuous growth necessitated the library's moving into five different locations before finding its home in the Family History Library on West Temple in Salt Lake City.

At this writing, the library, which is open to the general public at no charge, has an average of three thousand daily visitors, about 40 percent non-Mormon. These visitors can search the world's largest collection of genealogical records.

Today the microfilming of thousands of records is continuing on a large scale throughout the world. There are 250 full-time microfilm camera operators filming in forty-five different countries. The library has over 1,850,000 reels of microfilmed genealogical records. That's equal to almost seven million three-hundred-page bound volumes. The microfilm and volumes in the library contain over two billion names.

A powerful computer program, FamilySearch, enables visitors to quickly and easily search a collection of computer files containing information about 215 million deceased individuals from all over the world.

In addition, the Family History Library has a quarter of a million books in its collection and 2,200 branch libraries (called Family History Centers) in sixty countries.

It seems like such an overwhelming task to identify and provide temple ordinances for all of our ancestors back to Adam that one might wonder how we will ever succeed. Archibald F. Bennett reported that Susa Young Gates once asked her father, Brigham Young, how we would ever accomplish the great amount of temple work that must be done. Bennett wrote: "He told her there would be many inventions of labor-saving devices, so that our daily duties could be performed in a short time, leaving us more and more time for temple work. The inventions have come, and are still coming, but many simply divert the time gained to other channels, and not for the purpose intended by the Lord." ("Put on Thy Strength, O Zion!" *Improvement Era*, October 1952, p. 720.)

Computers, cars, microwaves—all these have come to help the Saints do this work. Elder Boyd K. Packer has testified: "When the servants of the Lord determine to do as He commands, we move ahead. As we proceed, we are joined at the crossroads by those who have been prepared to help us. They come with skills and abilities precisely suited to our needs. And we find provisions—information, inventions, help of various kinds—set along the way waiting for us to take them up. It is as though someone knew we would be traveling that way. We see the invisible hand of the Almighty providing for us." (*The Holy Temple* [Salt Lake City: Bookcraft, 1980], p. 182.)

One sister reported the experience she had with the Spirit of Elijah as follows:

> When my husband and I had been married for less than a month, he had to go through basic training and other training for the military. I was not allowed to accompany him, so for the six months he was gone I stayed in Provo, Utah, and worked. This was not my idea of married life—my husband over a thousand miles away and unable to come home for even a visit. I was a very unhappy bride.
>
> One night during this time, I was awakened from a deep sleep by a voice which came into my mind. As I listened to what was being said, I realized that my great-great-grandfather was speaking to me. I lay there for a moment, listening and thinking. My great-great-grandfather was telling me to have his family sealed to him. He had lived in the United States in the mid-1800s. Due to the Civil War and the economic conditions prior to the war, my great-great-grandfather George Wilkie had been away from his beloved wife and four sons a great deal. Eventually he died while serving his country in the Civil War.
>
> I had read copies of letters George Wilkie had written home to his family and letters his family had sent to him during his many absences. I had also read his journals. These letters and journals reflected the love family members had for one another, as well as their desires to be reunited.
>
> My ancestors were not LDS and did not have the blessings of the gospel. Now, in the middle of the night, here was my great-great-grandfather Wilkie saying to me, "Terry Lynn, please have my family sealed to me. I want to be with them through eternity. *Please* have our temple work done! You are now away from your husband—imagine that for eternity. It is

awful! I want to be sealed to my wife." Then, as suddenly as it had come, the voice was gone.

At first, I thought I must be imagining things, and I lay there and thought about my great-great-grandparents. I decided I should do their genealogy and would get to it when I had the time. Then I began to doze. I was startled when the voice returned and said much the same thing, only this time urging me to have the work done *soon*. I decided to do something about it the next day. Apparently, however, my grandfather knew I would probably be distracted the next day, because he spoke to me yet a third time, and told me to do something NOW!

I could not quite believe what was happening, but in the middle of the night I got up and began working on genealogy. I sorted through miscellaneous papers and records and found the information I needed to begin. I then wrote letters requesting birth, marriage, and death certificates. When I had done all that I could do at that time, I finally went back to bed.

I worked on genealogy a lot during the six months my husband was gone. Eventually, I was able to go to the temple with my cousin and have my great-great-grandparents sealed. I can testify that I felt their presence there in the temple and knew that, at last, they could be truly happy and together eternally.

Throughout the next four years my husband was required to be away from home much of the time. I was often comforted and strengthened reading the journals of my great-great-grandparents. Knowing that they had experienced similar situations somehow helped me to put my life in the proper perspective. I felt very close to them, and even though I had never met them, I felt I knew them. The example my great-great-grandparents unknowingly set for me has been, and continues to be, an inspiration. (Terry Lynn Fisher, "'Please Do My Work,'" *Ensign*, August 1983, pp. 54–55.)

Index

Grant, Emily Wells, 61
Grant, Heber J., 9, 61
Gratitude, 11–15

— H —

Handicaps, 68–70
Healings, 112
Hinckley, Bryant S., on Daniel H.
    Wells, 60–61
Hinckley, Gordon B., 53–54
*History of Joseph Smith by His
    Mother*, 25
Humility, 12
Huntington, Oliver B., on Zion's
    Camp, 44–45
Hymns, 46

— I —

Idaho Falls, 97–98
Idolatry, 101

— J —

Jackson County, Missouri, 33–35, 43
Jacob (Old Testament patriarch), 22
Jeroboam, 73
Jerusalem, protected by the Lord,
    118–19
Jesus Christ, atonement of, 82
    becoming like, 8
    gratitude for, 13
    keeper of the gate, 8–9
    often on mountaintops during
        mortal ministry, 19
    parables used by, 2

sacrifice required by, 61
seen in visions, 10, 49–51
testimony of, 19
See also God
Jews, 118–19, 122
Job, 79, 81
Jonah, 113–14
Joseph of Egypt, 26–27

— K —

Kendrick, L. Lionel, fisherman story
    related by, 116–17
Kimball, Heber C., 105–6
    on mob at Fishing River, 65–66
    spirit of discernment manifested
        by, 83–84
Kimball, Spencer W., on Abraham,
    13
    on sour grapes, 99–100
    on spirit of discernment, 83
    on wrestling for a blessing, 22–23
Kirtland, Ohio, 33, 43, 49, 62, 122

— L —

Lee, Harold B., on accepting call-
    ings, 63–64
Logan Temple, 83
Lot, 11–12

— M —

McConkie, Bruce R., on teaching
    with stories, 3
McKay, David O., 20
    vision of, 9–10